Job Interview Questior

M000222526

CORE **JAVA**

Interview Questions
You'll Most Likely Be Asked

367

Interview Questions

VIBRANT
PUBLISHERS

CORE **JAVA**
Interview Questions
You'll Most Likely Be Asked

ISBN-10: 1-946383-12-0
ISBN-13: 978-1-946383-12-9

Library of Congress Control Number: 2016920129

This publication is designed to provide accurate and authoritative information in regard to the subject matter covered. The author has made every effort in the preparation of this book to ensure the accuracy of the information. However, information in this book is sold without warranty either expressed or implied. The Author or the Publisher will not be liable for any damages caused or alleged to be caused either directly or indirectly by this book.

Vibrant Publishers books are available at special quantity discount for sales promotions, or for use in corporate training programs. For more information please write to **bulkorders@vibrantpublishers.com**

Please email feedback / corrections (technical, grammatical or spelling) to **spellerrors@vibrantpublishers.com**

To access the complete catalogue of Vibrant Publishers, visit **www.vibrantpublishers.com**

Table of Contents

This page is intentionally left blank.

CORE JAVA Interview Questions

Review these typical interview questions and think about how you would answer them. Read the answers listed; you will find best possible answers along with strategies and suggestions.

This page is intentionally left blank.

Chapter 1

Flow Controls and Assertions

1: What would be the output if boolA is false and boolB is true?

```
public void foo( boolean boolA, boolean boolB) /* Line 1 */
{
    if(boolA ) /* Line 3 */
    {
        System.out.println("X"); /* Line 5 */
    }
    else if(boolA && boolB) /* Line 7 */
    {
        System.out.println( "X && Y"); /* Line 9 */
    }
    else /* Line 11 */
    {
        if ( !boolB ) /* Line 13 */
        {
```

```
        System.out.println( "notY") ; /* Line 15 */
    }
    else /* Line 17 */
    {
        System.out.println( "In here" ) ; /* Line 19 */
    }
  }
}
```

Answer:

Output: In here

If boolA is false line 5 will never happen and X will not be printed. If boolA is false line 7 will also be false so X && Y will also not be printed. So the next option is line number 13. If boolB is true the condition is wrong and control goes to the else part and print "In here".

2: What will be the output?

```
public class SwitchTrial
{
    final static short caseVal = 2;
    public static void main(String [] abc)
    {
        for (int iterNo=0; iterNo < 3; iterNo ++)
        {
            switch (iterNo)
            {
                case caseVal: System.out.print("a ");
                case caseVal -1: System.out.print("b ");
```

case caseVal -2: System.out.print("c ");

      }

}

}

Answer:

Output: c b c a b c

Since caseVal is declared as a final variable, it can be evaluated at compile time. When interVal = 0, the 3rd case is true, caseVal – 2 = 0 so it prints c. Then in the 2nd iteration, iterVal becomes 1 so the 2nd case iterVal = caseVal – 1 is true so it prints B and the next one C. The 3rd time interval is 2 and the 1st case iterVal = caseVal = 2. So all a, b and c are printed. Then the loop exits.

3: What is an assertion in Java? How is it different from if – else conditions?

Answer:

An assertion is a Boolean expression which is assumed by the programme. If true it executes the next statement and if false the program throws an exception and ends. If - else conditions are different from the assertions as if the condition is false the else part takes over in if-else but in case of assertions, if the assert expression is false, the program ends throwing an error but will execute the second expression in assert statement.

Example:

```
public static void main(String [] abc)
{
        int var = 0;
        System.out.println("Enter a value bigger than 20 : ");
```

```
        var = in.nextLine();
        assert var / 2 >5 : System.out.println("Please try again and
        enter the correct value");
        System.out.println("Good Choice!");
}
```

Case 1:

Enter a value bigger than 20: 10

Exception in thread "main" java.lang.AssertionError: *Please try again and enter the correct value*

Case 2:

Enter a value bigger than 20: 30

Good Choice!

When Case 1 executes the output will be - Exception in thread "main" java.lang.AssertionError: *Please try again and enter the correct value*. Case 2 will not throw any exception as the assumption or assertion is true and hence the next line in program will execute and the output is Good Choice!

4: What are called Decision statements in Java?

Answer:

The Decision statement is a statement which evaluates a given expression and based on the logical result, performs the execution. There are two decision statements in Java. They are:

a) if

b) switch

5: What are the looping constructs in Java?

Answer:

Looping constructs are statements which are executed again and again based on the logical result. Java has three types of looping constructs. They are

a) for

b) while

c) do

6: How will you legally define "if else" statement. Give an example.

Answer:

The valid format of "if else" statement is described below:

```
If(iValue > 1000) {
        System.out.println("iValue is > 1000");
}
else {
        System.out.println("iValue is < 1000");
}
```

7: What happens when you execute the code below? If it compiles, what will be the output?

```
int iValue1 = 100;
int iValue2 = 200;


boolean isTrue() {
        return true;
}
```

```
if(((iValue1 > iValu2) && (iValue2 < 50)) | isTrue()) {
        System.out.println("This is True");
}
else {
        System.out.println("This is False");
}
```

Answer:

The code compiles just fine and it displays the below output:

        This is True

It is because, isTrue() method returns TRUE and the &&
expression returns FALSE. The | returns TRUE for FALSE TRUE
combination.

8: What is the use of "break" and "continue" statements?

Answer:

As the name implies, the keyword "break" is used to stop
executing the statement and come out of the loop.

The "continue" keyword is used to stop executing the next
statement and continue executing the first statement below the
loop.

**9: What happens when you compile and execute the code below?
What will be the output?**

```
for(int iValue=0; iValue<5; iValue++) {
        System.out.println(iValue);
        continue;
        System.out.println(iValue + 1);
}
```

Answer:

The code compiles and on executing it displays the below output:

    0

    1

    2

    3

    4

It is because "continue" statement will stop executing the next statement and start executing the first statement of the loop.

10: What happens when you compile and execute the code below? What will be the output?

```
for(int iValue=0; iValue<5; iValue++) {
        System.out.println(iValue);
        break;
        System.out.println(iValue + 1);
}
```

Answer:

The code compiles and on executing it displays the below output:

    0

It prints just 0 because the break statement will stop executing the next statement and push you out of the loop.

11: What happens when you compile and execute the code below? What will be the output?

```
for (;;) {
        System.out.println("Will this get printed?");
}
```

Answer:

The above mentioned code compiles fine but it never stops executing. This is because it is an infinite loop and keeps on printing the output "Will this get printed?".

12: What happens when you compile and execute the code below? What will be the output?

```
int iValue = 50;
for (;iValue < 100;) {
        System.out.println(iValue);
}
```

Answer:

Compilation and execution will be successful and display the output from 50 to 99.

Output:

50

51

...

99

13: What is the benefit of enhanced "for" loop?

Answer:

The enhanced "for" loop is mainly used to loop through an array object or a collection object. It is introduced in Java 5 and the valid format is described as below:

        for (Declaration : Expression)

The Declaration must be a type that you assign based on the expression type.

The Expression can be of the following:

a) Array variable

b) Call to a method that returns an array

Also, the array can be a primitive, an object or an array of arrays.

14: How will you declare a valid enhanced "for" loop?

Answer:

A valid enhanced "for" loop is described below:

```
Integer [] integerArray = {10, 100, 1000};
for(Integer integer : integerArray) {}


int [] iValue = {10, 100, 1000};
for(int iValue1 : iValue) {}


Electronics [] electronics = {new Camera(), new Laptop()};
for(Electronics e : electronics) {}
```

15: What will be the output of the following code?

```
for(int iValue = 0; iValue < 10; iValue++) {}
System.out.println(iValue);
```

Answer:

The above mentioned code will not compile. It is because the variable 'iValue' scope is available only within the "for" loop and not beyond the "for" loop.

16: Which lines of below code will compile and which will not?

```
while (iValue) {} //Line 1
while (false) {} //Line 2
```

while (iValue = 5) {} //Line 3

while (iValue == 5) {} //Line 4

Answer:

Line 1 and Line 3 will not get compiled.

Line 2 and Line 4 gets compiled.

It is because the return type of an expression must be a boolean.

17: Look at the code below. What will happen when you execute the below code? If it compiles fine, what will be the output?

```
int iValue = 10;
switch(iValue) {
        case 5: System.out.println("5");
        case 8: System.out.println("5");
        default: System.out.println("This is Default");
        case 9: { System.out.println("9"); break; }
        case 11: System.out.println("11");
}
```

Answer:

The above mentioned code compiles fine and displays the below output.

> This is Default
>
> 9

Although 10 is not available, "default" it gets executed and executes the next statement as well. The code will not print 11. It's because of the "break" statement.

18: What are the benefits of assertions?

Answer:

Below are the benefits of Assertions:

a) It is used to test your logical assumptions when you develop your code.

For example:

```
if(intNumber >= 0) {
        invokeMethod(intNumber);
}
```

We are not supposed to make assumptions. It is not the case when you write code. So, the above piece of code can be written as

```
assert(intNumber >= 0);
invokeMethod(intNumber);
```

b) It is also useful to write the code clean and we have the option of turning the assertions on and off. i.e., if we know that the above assumption is correct in all the scenarios, then we don't need to write the exception handling code. Also, to enable assertion in the code, we have to use the assert keyword.

19: When will you use assertions?

Answer:

Assertions should be used only while developing your application. It should be tuned OFF when you deploy your application. We have the option of enabling assertion even though the application is deployed but it is mainly used for testing purpose.

20: How will you use assertion?

Answer:

Assertion can be used with the help of "assert" keyword. We can use assertions either as an identifier or as a keyword as described in the below code. But it cannot be used both as an identifier and as a keyword.

```
float assert = getFloat();
if(assert == getFloatValue()) { }
        (OR)
assert (iValue1 > iValue2);
```

21: Which of the following codes are legal?

```
int iValue1 = 1;
int iValue2 = 2;
boolean bValue = false;
assert(iValue > iValue2) : "iValue1 : "+ iValue1 + "iValue2 : " +
iValue2); //Line 1
assert(iValue1) : iValue2; //Line 2
assert(bValue); //Line 3
assert(iValue2 == 1) : new Electronics(); //Line 4
assertiValue == 2) : callMethod(); //Line 5
assert 0; //Line 6
asset(iValue == 2) : ; //Line 7
```

Answer:

Lines 1, 3, 4, and 5 are legal and gets compiled fine because each of the statements return a value.

Line 2, 6, and 7 are illegal and will not compile because they are not 'boolean' and they do not return a value.

22: Which of the Java versions support assertion?

Answer:

Assertion is introduced and supported in Java 1.4. The previous versions are not supported for assertion but they give warnings and compilation error.

23: How will you compile your Java code for assertions?

Answer:

The below command is used to compile the Java code:

    javac –source 6 com.resource.Electronics.java

    javac –source 1.5 com.resource.Electronics.java

We can use 1.5 or just 5 and similarly 1.6 or just 6 in the above command.

24: How will you enable and disable assertion for your class during runtime?

Answer:

Assertion is enabled from command line when you execute your code:

        java –enableassertions com.resource.Electronics

        (OR)

        java –ea com.resource.Electronics

Assertion is disabled from command line when you execute your code:

        java –disableassertions com.resource.Electronics

        (OR)

        java –da com.resource.Electronics

25: How will you enable and disable assertion for a package during runtime?

Answer:

Assertion is enabled and disabled for a package as below:

    java –ea com.resource...

    java –da com.resource...

26: What does the below line of code represent?

java –ea –dsa

Answer:

The above code implies that assertion is enabled during runtime for general cases but assertion is disabled for system classes i.e., assertion is disabled for all the classes and interfaces that are available in Java API.

27: What does the below line of code represent?

java –ea –da:com.resource...

Answer:

The above code implies that assertion is enabled during runtime for general cases but assertion is disabled specifically for the package called resource.

28: When to use assertions in public method and when to not? In general, what is the best practice?

Answer:

The best practice is to use assertion only in private methods. Assertions can be used in 'public' method only to validate the execution of the block of code. Example:

```
Public void my_assertCall(int my_inum1){
        assert(my_isTrue1());
        My_inum1 = my_inum1 * 99; // Line 2
}
public boolean my_isTrue1(){
        return false;
}
```

Based on the value returned by the my_isTrue1(), Line2 gets executed. When the my_isTrue1() returns 'True', Line 2 gets executed, else the assert function throws error causing the execution to halt.

This page is intentionally left blank.

Chapter 2

Wrapper Classes, Garbage Collection and Exception Handling

29: What is a Wrapper class in Java? What are the special properties of Wrapper class objects?

Answer:

Java is completely Object Oriented so everything in Java should correspond to an Object. But the primitives in Java are not objects. So the wrapper classes convert Java Primitives to corresponding Objects so that they can be utilized in the programs. Each primitive has a corresponding wrapper class and you can create an object of that type. In the same way you can convert a wrapper object to the primitive type too. If you have an integer variable in Java, you can convert it into an Integer object using a wrapper class. Similarly you can convert an Integer object to int primitive type also. All wrapper objects are final. So you cannot extend the wrapper classes.

30: What will be the output?

```
public class MyTrialBoolean {
    public static void main(String a[]){
        //create Boolean using boolean primitive type
        boolean boo1 = true;

        Boolean booObj1 = new Boolean (boo1);
        System.out.println("Wrapper class Boolean output: "+booObj1);

        Boolean booObj2 = new Boolean ("false"); //create
        Boolean using string value
        System.out.println("Wrapper class Boolean output: "+booObj2);

        // booleanValue() returns the primitive Boolean value
        from wrapper class
        System.out.println(booObj1.booleanValue());
    }
}
```

Answer:

The output will be

Wrapper class Boolean output: true

Wrapper class Boolean output: false

true

31: What is Garbage Collection in Java?

Answer:

Garbage collection is the process of freeing the memory allocated to objects that are no longer used. During runtime, when an object is created, the JVM allocates some memory to hold the object which can be referenced later. The JVM periodically checked for the objects in use and de-allocates the memory for those objects which are not in use anymore. Garbage collection is this process of removing objects no longer in use. So the programmer does not have to bother about manual de-allocation of memory.

32: Which part of the memory is used in Garbage Collection? Which algorithm does the JVM use for Garbage collection?

Answer:

Garbage Collection is done in the Heap Memory. The JVM uses the mark and swap algorithm internally for garbage collection.

33: Can you guarantee or force Garbage Collection? If so explain how?

Answer:

Java does not guarantee Garbage Collection though it keeps trying. You cannot force the JVM to do garbage collection but can request the same by invoking the gc() method. We can invoke the gc() method in 2 ways:

    a) Runtime.getRuntime().gc()

    b) System.gc()

Either ways garbage collection still cannot be guaranteed.

34: What is the difference between an error and an exception in Java?

Answer:

Errors are irrecoverable whereas Exceptions can be handled. Usually when there's an error, the program ends abruptly. If it is an exception which is handled, the instructions in the exception handling part of the program will be executed.

35: Explain 'throw', 'throws' and 'Throwable' in Java.

Answer:

The 'throws' keyword is used to specify that a particular method throws an unhandled exception or multiple exceptions which need to be handled separately. In some other method or later in the program this exception has to be handled using a try-catch-finally block.

The 'throw' keyword is used inside that method to explicitly throw an exception. This is usually the after effect of some condition that does not satisfy.

'Throwable' is the base class of Errors and Exceptions. You can create a User Defined Exception by extending the 'Throwable' class.

36: Explain the try-catch-finally statement in Java.

Answer:

The Try-Catch-Finally statement is what allows exception handling in Java. You can put the statements that have a tendency to throw exception like user inputs. In case the user inputs are wrong or go beyond the allowed values and the exception is thrown, the catch section will handle that exception. Depending on the type of exception thrown, the set of statements within that catch exception will be executed. The "Finally" block is at all times executed irrespective of whether an exception is thrown or not.

```
try {
// Statements to be executed
}
catch (ExceptionType 1) {
// Instructions to follow if an exception occurs
}
catch (ExceptionType 2) {
// Instructions to follow if an exception occurs
}
catch (ExceptionType n) {
// Instructions to follow if an exception occurs
}
finally {
// this block is definitely executed even if an exception is thrown
or not
}
```

37: What is the output?

```
public class sampleMultipleException {
    public static void main(String abc[]){
        try{
            int no = new int;
```

```
            no = 52/0;
    }
    catch(ArithmeticException aE){ // checking specific exception
            System.out.println("Number");
    }
    catch(ArrayIndexOutOfBoundsException aOBE){ //
    checking specific exception
            System.out.println("Array Out Of Bound");
    }
    catch(Exception e){  // any other exception
            System.out.println("Sorry Unhandled Exception");
    }
    finally { // this will be executed
            System.out.println("I am done!");
    }


            System.out.println("Thank You!!");
    }
}
```

Answer:

This program will give the following output:

Number

I am done!

Thank You!!

38: What is the purpose of wrapper classes?

Answer:

Wrapper classes are mainly used for two purposes.

a)   It is used to wrap the primitive values to an object.

Example: Adding a primitive to a Collection.

b) It is also used for conversion of primitive to String and vice versa as it provides many functions.

39: What are the wrapper classes available in Java?

Answer:

Below are the wrapper classes available in Java:

a) **Byte:** This takes a byte or String as an argument

b) **Short:** This takes short or String as an argument

c) **Integer:** This takes int or String as an argument

d) **Long:** This takes long or String as an argument

e) **Float:** This takes float, double or String as an argument

f) **Double:** This takes double or String as an argument

g) **Character:** This takes char as an argument

h) **Boolean:** This takes boolean or String as an argument

So, all of the wrapper classes take their primitive type or String as an argument except Character as it takes only char (its primitive type) as an argument.

40: How will you define Autoboxing with an example?

Answer:

Autoboxing referred as Boxing or Unboxing is a feature introduced in Java 5 which helps programmers to reduce some lines of code. For example, the wrapper classes, in order to be assigned to a primitive, require unwrapping, using, and re-wrapping which is not required now with the help of Autoboxing.

Without Autoboxing:

Integer integerValue = new Integer(1000);

Int iValue = integerValue.intValue(); //unwrapping

iValue ++; //Using

integerValue = new Ineger(iValue); //re-wrapping

With Autoboxing:

Integer integerValue = new Integer(1000);

integerValue ++;

In the above scenario, for both cases, the value of integerValue is 1001.

41: What will be the output when you execute the below code?

```
class Test {
        static Integer integerValue;
        public static void main (String arg[]) {
                callMethod(integerValue);
        }
        static void callMethod(int iValue) {
                System.out.println(100 + iValue);
        }
}
```

Answer:

The above code compiles fine but NullPointerException is thrown by JVM (Java Virtual Machine) during runtime because, we cannot pass an Integer value to a method that accepts int.

42: Explain how will you convert a String "100.55" to a Double

and a Double 100.55 to a String?

Answer:

We can convert a String to a Double with the help of
Double.parseDouble() method as below:

Double doubleValue = Double.parseDouble("100.55");

We can convert a Double to a String with the help of
Double.toString() method as below:

String stringValue = Double.toString(100.55);

43: What will be the output of "doubleValue" on executing the below mentioned code?

Double doubleValue = Double.parseDouble("Java");

Answer:

The above code compiles just fine but it throws the below
exception:

NumberFormatException

This is because JVM cannot convert the String to Double as it does
not fall within the expected range.

44: Assume that you have a method callMe() which is overloaded in a Class. In one case, it accepts an Integer as argument and in another case, it accepts Long as argument. What will happen if you pass an int value and try to call the method? Will that code compile? If so, which method will be invoked?

Answer:

From the above description, we have two methods:

callMe(Integer integerValue)

callMe(Long longValue)

We also have int:

int i = 10;

We are trying to invoke a method by passing the int value like below:

callMe(i)

In the above scenario, the method callMe(Long longValue) will be invoked. This is because JVM uses the Widening (choosing the maximum range of bytes the data type holds) feature which overcomes the Boxing (converting primitive to wrapper and vice versa) feature.

45: What are the features we need to know while invoking overloaded methods?

Answer:

We need to understand three features while invoking overloaded methods. They are

a) **Widening:** This feature always chooses the maximum range of bytes. For example, Long type holds maximum amount of bytes than Integer.

b) **Autoboxing:** This feature converts the primitive to wrapper and vice versa.

c) **Var-args:** Using this feature, we can pass multiple arguments to a method by passing single argument with three dots as shown below:

public static String invokeFormat(String strPattern,Object... myArgs);

As per the above order, Widening overcomes Autoboxing and

Var-Args and Autoboxing overcomes Var-args.

46: How will you define Garbage Collection?

Answer:

Garbage collection is an automatic feature which takes care of memory management in Java.

Whenever the objects are declared null or if the objects are no longer used in a program, the Java Virtual machine clears those objects from memory and thereby make the system clean.

47: When does the garbage collection get executed?

Answer:

The JVM (Java Virtual Machine) controls garbage collection. So, the JVM decides when to execute garbage collection.

It is possible to invoke garbage collection through Java program. But there is no guarantee that the garbage collection is executed by JVM when the program is triggered.

The JVM triggers garbage collection only if an object is assigned a null value or if the objects are no longer used.

48: Is there any chance that the Java application can throw "out of memory" error? Why?

Answer:

Yes, a Java application can throw "out of memory" error. This is because whenever the objects are not used, garbage collector removes those objects. But if there are many objects live then the Java application can run out of memory.

49: Explain with a code sample when an object is ready for garbage collection.

Answer:

An object will be garbage collected when it is no longer used.

For example:

String stringValue = "This is a String value"; //Line 1

stringValue = null; //Line 2

Once Line 2 is executed, the object stringValue will be removed from memory by the garbage collector.

50: What are the situations in which JVM triggers garbage collection?

Answer:

There are three situations in which JVM triggers garbage collection. They are:

a) When you make the reference variable as null

For example:

String strName = null;

b) When you re-assign a reference variable

For example:

String strName1 = "Name 1";

String strName2 = "Name 2";

strName1 = strName2;

c) When you isolate a reference variable

For example:

MyClass m;

MyClass mc = new MyClass();

MyClass ms = new MyClass();

MyClass my = new MyClass();

mc.m = ms;

ms.i = my;

my.i = mc;

51: What are the lines of code you need to write to programmatically trigger garbage collection?

Answer:

The below lines of code have to be written to trigger garbage collection:

Runtime runTime = Runtime.getRuntime();

runTime.gc();

The RunTime class is a special class which has a feature that can directly communicate with the Virtual machine by using the gc() method.

52: What are the concepts that come to your mind about finalize() method?

Answer:

There are two important concepts about finalize() method.

a)   The garbage collector triggers the finalize() method only once.

b)   If you invoke finalize() programmatically, the nullified reference object might not be deleted.

53: What is the recommended way of programmatically calling Garbage collector?

Answer:

a) Using 'gc' function. gc function in both System and Runtime class can be used

b) This function gets executed based on the 'Java Heap Size'. Java Virtual Machine triggers this function when garbage collection is needed

Example:

System/Runtime.gc()

54: How will you define Exception Handling?

Answer:

Exception handling is a mechanism through which we can handle Java Run time errors.

It is an organized and efficient way of handling errors in Java through which you can reduce 20% of your development time as 20% of time is spend for code debugging.

We can handle exceptions in Java code using any of the following keywords: try, catch, throw, throws, and finally.

55: What are the different types of Exceptions?

Answer:

There are three types of exceptions we need to take care of. They are:

a) **Runtime Exception or Unchecked Exception:** These type of exceptions occur during run time as we don't write code to handle exceptions

b) **Checked Exception:** These types of exceptions are handled using try, catch, finally, throw or throws keyword.

c) **Error:** It is the behavior which stops the working of the system during program execution.

56: How will you handle Exception in Java?

Answer:

We can handle exception in the following two ways:

a) Use "try", "catch", and "finally" blocks in your code

For example:

```
try {
        // Code comes here
} catch(Exception exp) {
        System.out.println("Exception: "+exp);
} finally {
        System.out.println("This is always executed");
}
```

b) Use "throws" or "throw" clause to throw the exception in the server log

For example:

```
public void myMethod() throws MyNewException {
        try {
                throw new MyNewException();
        } catch(Exception exp) {}
}
```

57: What will be the output when you compile and execute the following code?

```
class Test {
        try {
```

```
    System.out.println("This is try block");
}

    System.out.println("Try block is executed"); //Line 1
    catch(Exception exp) {
        System.out.println("This is catch block");
    }

}
```

Answer:

The above code will not compile and will throw compilation error. This is because, if you look at the code at Line 1, the code is written after the end of try block. The rule is that we have to write code either inside try block or inside catch block but not in-between.

58: Write a compilable code using "try"," catch", and "finally".

Answer:

Following is a way to use "try", "catch", and "finally" in Java code.

```
    class Test {
        try {
                System.out.println("This is try block");
        } catch {
                System.out.println("This is catch block");
        }
        finally {
                System.out.println("This is finally block");
        }
    }
```

59: What is the use of "finally" clause? Give an example.

Answer:

The "finally" clause is mainly used to clean up the code when exception occur during code execution. The "finally" block is the one which gets executed when the exception occurs during run time.

For example, we open a DB connection to fetch records from database. It might throw number format exception, if data in DB is improper and the code will end abruptly without closing the DB connection. In such an instance, we have to use "finally" clause to close the DB connection.

60: What will be the output on executing the below mentioned code?

```
class ExceptionTest {
        public static void main(String argument[]) {
                callMethod();
        }
        static void callMethod() {
                int intValue = 100 / 0;
                System.out.println("intValue is: "+intValue);
        }
}
```

Answer:

The above code gets compiled without an issue but on executing it throws "Arithmetic Exception" with the long stack trace (Error information or report) in the server log as shown below:

Exception in thread "main" java.lang.ArithmeticException: / by zero

at ExceptionTest.callMethod(ExceptionTest.java:12)

at ExceptionTest.main(ExceptionTest.java:9)

61: What are the exception types that can be thrown using the "throw" keyword?

Answer:

There are four types of exceptions we can throw using "throw" keyword. They are:

a) **Throwable:** It is the super class of all the errors and exception.

b) **Error:** These are compile time errors that pop up during compilation.

c) **Exception:** These are run time errors that pop up during program execution. It is the sub class of Throwable class.

d) **RunTimeException:** It is the sub class of Exception class which throws all the exceptions that are thrown by the Java Virtual machine during program execution.

62: How will you write a compilable code block using "throw" keyword?

Answer:

Below is the compilable code block which uses "throw" keyword:

```
class ExceptionTest { // Line 1
        public static void main(String argument[]) {
                callMethod();
        }
        static void callMethod() { //Line 2
```

```
try {
        throw new Error(); //Line 3
} catch(Error error) {
        throw error; //Catch it and re-throw it
    }
  }
}
```

In the above code, we have thrown Error() in Line 3. If we have used Exception() instead of Error() in Line 3, then we must have to extend the Exception class in Line 1 and also use throw keyword on the method declaration in Line 2.

This page is intentionally left blank.

Chapter 3

Threads

63: Differentiate between a Thread and a Process in Java.

Answer:

A Thread is the path a particular process is running in. A process is a section of a program which is being executed.

64: What are the different types of Thread? Explain.

Answer:

Threads are of 2 types – Daemon Threads and Non-Daemon Threads.

All user defined threads are Non-Daemon Threads unless they are explicitly set to be a Daemon thread. Daemon threads are usually used for background processes such as Garbage Collection. As soon as all Non-Daemon threads stop running, the JVM stops running and does not wait for the Daemon threads to stop.

65: What is a deadlock in Java and how do you avoid it?

Answer:

A deadlock happens when one thread is holding on to an object waiting to be accessed in another thread and the other thread is waiting for the access of the object on hold in the first thread.

T1 wants Obj1 and is holding Obj2

T2 wants Obj2 and is holding Obj1

This results in a deadlock.

To avoid deadlock, depending on what gets the code to enter a deadlock the solution can be provided. An ordered and synchronized access to objects can avoid deadlocks to a great extend.

66: What is the difference between wait() and sleep()?

Answer:

The sleep(n) asks the thread to wait for a specific amount of time. The thread wakes up exactly after the specified amount of time. The wait(x) method keeps the thread waiting for maximum specified amount of time. It may be invoked by a notify() or notifyAll() method anytime before the specified time.

67: The start() method is usually called in the thread which in turn calls the run() method. Why is usually the run() method called directly?

Answer:

The start() method creates a new thread and runs the process there, whereas the run() method just runs the process in the same thread.

68: How will you define a Thread?

Answer:

Thread is an object which is used to perform more than one task simultaneously. In a Java program, we can implement more than one thread through which we can perform multitasking. For example, assume that one task writes streams of contents in a file and another task loads an application and display the pages. Using threads, we can perform both the tasks simultaneously.

69: What happens behind the scenes when you execute the below program?

```
class Test {
        public static void main(String argument[]) {
                System.out.println("Thread Example...");
        }
}
```

Answer:

When the above program is executed, the JVM creates the main thread automatically. When the main thread stops, the program terminates.

70: How will you create Threads in Java?

Answer:

We can create threads in two ways as described below:

a) By extending "Thread" class

b) By implementing the interface called "Runnable"

71: What are the methods of Thread class that are mainly used to manage threads?

Answer:

a) **start():** Initiate the thread and invoke the run() method

b) **run():** Task to be performed is declared inside run() method

c) **sleep():** makes the running process to wait for a particular time

d) **yield():** makes the waiting threads to run if the current thread is running without a break

e) **stop():** Stop the thread execution permanently

f) **join():** link another thread

g) **isAlive():** Returns true if thread passed to it is running, else false

h) **setPriority():** Set the priority of the thread

72: How does a thread get executed in Java?

Answer:

a) Java Virtual Machine initiates the main thread whenever a Java program is executed

b) All the child threads are contained in the 'main thread'

c) 'start' method triggers the thread and that in turn calls the 'run'method

d) Run method starts the thread and performs the execution

73: What are the thread states?

Answer:

Thread exists in five states. They are:

a) **New:** When the thread is initiated, it enters the New state

b) **Runnable:** When the run() method is invoked, then the thread is ready to execute the particular task. This state is called as Runnable state.

c) **Running:** When the thread execute a particular task then it is said to be in Running state

d) **Waiting / Blocking:** When the thread is made to wait for a certain time, then it enters the Waiting state

e) **Dead:** When the thread completes the execution it enters the Dead state

74: Write a compilable Java code that creates a child thread using "Thread" class.

Answer:

The following code creates a child thread using "Thread" class :

```
class TestForThread extends Thread {
    public static void main(String argument[]) {
        TestForThread thread = new TestForThread();
        thread.start(); // Line 1
    }
    public void run() {
        System.out.println("Inside Run Method..");// Line 2
    }
}
```

In the above code, whenever Line 1 is executed, a child thread is created and it executes the steps that are mentioned inside the run() method.

75: What are the methods of Objects that are used while managing threads?

Answer:

There are three methods of Objects that are used while managing threads. They are

a) **wait():** This will make the thread to wait until it is invoked by notify() method.

b) **notify():** This method starts the execution of a particular waiting thread

c) **notifyAll():** This method starts the execution of all the waiting threads

The access modifiers for all the above methods are by default 'public' and 'final'. The wait() method throws an InterruptedException when the method is invoked.

76: Write a compilable Java code that creates a child thread using "Runnable".

Answer:

The following code creates a child thread by implementing "Runnable" Interface:

```
class TestForThread implements Runnable { //Line 1
        public static void main(String argument[]) {
                TestForThread myThread = new TestForThread();
                Thread thread = new Thread(myThread);
                thread.start(); // Line 2
        }
        public void run() {
                System.out.println("Inside Run Method..");
```

```
    }

}
```

In the above code, in Line 1, we have implemented the Runnable interface using the implements keyword and whenever Line 2 is executed, the child thread is created in the memory.

77: Is it possible to create more than one thread in a Java application? If so, how will the threads communicate with each other?

Answer:

Yes, it is possible to create more than one thread in a Java application. For two threads to communicate with each other, we have to use the object methods namely wait(), notify(), and notifyAll().

For example, assume that we have an order collection process thread and a delivery thread. Delivery thread has to be triggered only if the collection process thread receives order. The collection process cannot look for the order all the time so we use wait() method to look for a particular time and once we receive the order, we use notify() or notifyAll() method to trigger delivery.

78: How will you define Synchronization?

Answer:

Synchronization is a locking mechanism which is used to control the threads. For example, if multiple threads try to access a shared resource at the same time, then we need some way for the resource to be accessed by only one Thread at a time. So, the main purpose of Synchronization is to protect and secure data.

79: What will happen when you execute the code below?

Runnable runnable = new Runnable();

Runnable.run();

Answer:

a) Compilation and execution will be successful. This creates an object ' runnable' for the class 'Runnable' that implements 'Runnable'and calls the function 'run' that executes in current thread.

b) This does not create a new thread.

c) To create a new thread,

     Runnable my_runnable1 = new Runnable();

     Thread my_thrd1 = new Thread(my_runnable1);

     my_thrd1.start();

80: Look at the code below. What will happen when you execute the below code? If it compiles fine, what will be the output?

```
class TestMyRunnable implements Runnable {
    public void run() {
        System.out.println("Inside Run Method..");
        System.out.println("Name of thread is:
        "+Thread.currentThread().getName());
    }
}
class TestMyThread {
    public static void main(String argument[]) {
        TestMyRunnable runnable = new TestMyRunnable();
        Thread thread = new Thread(runnable);
        Thread.setName("My Thread");
        thread.start(); //Line 1
```

```
        }
}
```

Answer:

The above mentioned code compiles fine and displays the below output.

Inside Run Method.

Name of thread is: My Thread

Whenever Line 1 is executed, it invokes the run() method. The run() method executes the print statement and displays the thread name using Thread's getName() method.

81: Look at the code below. What will happen when you execute the below code? If it compiles fine, what will be the output?

```
class TestMyRunnable implements Runnable {
        public void run() {
                System.out.println("Inside Run Method..");
                        System.out.println("Name of thread is:
                        "+Thread.currentThread().getName());
        }
        public static void main(String argument[]) {
                TestMyRunnable runnable = new
                TestMyRunnable();
                Thread thread = new Thread(runnable); // Line 1
                thread.start(); //Line 2
        }
}
```

Answer:

The above mentioned code compiles fine and displays the below output.

Inside Run Method.

Name of thread is: Thread-0

In the above code, the thread object 'thread' is created in Line 1 and is initiated in Line 2. The Line 2 then invokes the run() method which executes the print statements and displays the output.

82: What will be the output for the following code?

```java
class TestMyMain {
        public static void main(String argument[]) {
                System.out.println("Name of thread is:
                "+Thread.currentThread().getName(); // Line 1
        }
}
```

Answer:

The above mentioned code compiles fine and displays the following output.

Name of thread is: main

It is because, whenever the Java Virtual Machine execute Line 1, it knows that the line is inside the main method. Since the "main" method is a thread and it has a name called "main", the value "main" is displayed in the console.

83: Look at the code below.

```java
class TestMyRunnable implements Runnable {
    public void run() {
        for(int iValue = 0; iValue < 1000; iValue++)
```

```
        System.out.println("Name of thread is:
        "+Thread.currentThread().getName());

    }

    public static void main(String argument[]) {
        TestMyRunnable runnable = new TestMyRunnable();
        Thread threadC = new Thread(runnable);
        Thread threadD = new Thread(runnable);
        threadC.setName("Thread 1");
        threadD.setName("Thread 2");
        threadC.start();
        threadD.start();
    }

}
```

Executing the above code first prints the Thread one thousand times and then prints the Thread two thousand times. If this is incorrect, explain the reasons.

Answer:

On executing the above mentioned code, it will not print the Thread one thousand times and then the Thread two thousand times. We really don't know what will be the order in which it will get printed and which Thread finishes first, as the scheduler handles this scenario of group of threads and we don't have control on the scheduler.

84: How will you make a thread to pause for ten minutes?

Answer:

We can make a thread to enter into sleep mode for ten minutes by invoking the sleep() method. Below is the code which makes a thread to pause or sleep for 10 minutes.

```
try {
        Thread.sleep(10 * 60 * 1000)
}
catch(InterruptedException exp) {
}
```

85: How will you use the "synchronized" keyword? Give code examples.

Answer:

We can use the "synchronized" keyword only for blocks of code and for methods. We cannot use "synchronized" keyword for classes and variables.

For example:

```
public void callMethod1() {
        System.out.println("This is not synchronized");
        synchronized(this) {
                System.out.println("This is synchronized");
        }
}
public synchronized void callMethod2() {
        System.out.println("This is synchronized");
}
```

86: What happens when a synchronized method is invoked?

Answer:

Whenever the synchronized method is executed, the thread enters into the monitor or lock mode and until the method gets executed the lock is not released. So, using synchronized method, we allow one thread to access the shared resource when multiple threads are running simultaneously and trying to access a shared resource.

87: How will you make the thread to wait and start its execution again so that certain process gets executed?

Answer:

We have to use the wait() method to make the thread to wait.

For example:

```
synchronized(threadY) {
        try {
                system.out.println("Calling wait...");
                threadY.wait(); // Line 1
        }
        catch (Exception exp) {}
                System.out.println("iTotal is : "+threadY.iTotal);
}
```

In the above code, in Line 1, we made the threadY to wait using the wait() method.

We have to use the notify() or notifyAll() method for the thread to start its execution again.

For example:

```
synchronized(this) {
        for(int iValue=0;iValue<1000;iValue++) {
                iTotal = iTotal + iValue;
        }
        notify(); //Line 1
```

```
}
```

In the above code, when Line 1 is executed, it starts executing the thread which is forced to wait.

88: Write a Java code and implement "wait" and "notify" methods.

Answer:

The "wait" and "notify" methods must always be implemented within a synchronized block. The below code explains the same:

```
class ThreadX {
    public static void main(string argument[]) {
        ThreadY threadY = new ThreadY();
        threadY.start();
        synchronized(threadY) {
            try {
                system.out.println("Calling wait...");
                threadY.wait();
            }
            catch (Exception exp) {}
                System.out.println("iTotal is :
                "+threadY.iTotal);
        }
    }
}
class ThreadY {
    int iTotal ;
    public void run() {
        synchronized(this) {
            for(int iValue=0;iValue<1000;iValue++) {
```

```
            iTotal = iTotal + iValue;
        }
        notify();
      }
    }
}
```

Since the access modifiers of wait() and notify() methods are public and final, we have to implement these methods within the synchronized block as mentioned in the above code.

89: What is a Deadlock?

Answer:

Deadlock is a scenario which occurs when two or more threads wait for other thread's lock to get released. When one thread gets locked, the other locked thread will never be able to access the first thread object until the first thread gives up the lock.

For example, look at the below code:

```
public class DeadlockExample {
    public static class Test1 {
        public int iValue;
    }
    public Test1 t1 = new Test1();
    public Test1 t2 = new Test1();
    public void callMe() {
        synchronized(t2) { //Line 1
            synchronized (t1) {
                t1.iValue1 = 1000;
                t2.iValue1 = 2000;
```

}
}
}
}

In the above code, deadlock happens when line 1 is executed.

90: When will Deadlock happen?

Answer:

The Deadlock happens as explained in the below scenario:

a) Thread 1 triggers synchronized block and gets locked

b) In the next line, it triggers another synchronized block and tries to access the objects of locked thread

For example, look at the below code:

```
public void callMe() {
    synchronized(t2) {
        synchronized (t1) {
            t1.iValue1 = 1000; //Line 1
            t2.iValue1 = 2000;
        }
    }
}
```

In the above code, lead lock happens at Line 1 because the second locked thread is trying to access the object of first locked thread.

91: What are the methods that belong to "Runnable" interface?
Answer:

The "Runnable" interface has only one method called run(). We need to call the method run() from the thread class using the method start(). If we invoke the method run() as mentioned in the below code, thread will not be created.

```
class TestMyRunnable implements Runnable {
        public void run() {
                        System.out.println("This gets printed");
        }
        public static void main(String argument[]) {
                        TestMyRunnable runnable = new
                        TestMyRunnable();
                        Thread threadC = new Thread(runnable);
                        threadC.run(); //Line1
        }
}
```

In the above code, we have invoked run() method in Line 1 which will not create a thread. So, to create thread, we have to modify the Line 1 as threadC.start().

92: What is the use of join() and yield() methods?

Answer:

The join() method is mainly used to instruct the next line to wait until the currently executing thread finishes executing.

For example, if threadA and threadB are executing simultaneously and if threadB invokes the join() method, it instructs threadA to wait until threadB finished executing.

The yield() method is mainly used to pause the currently executing thread and allow the other thread to execute.

For example, if threadA and threadB are executing simultaneously and if threadB invokes the yield() method, it allows threadA to execute and wait until threadA finished executing.

This page is intentionally left blank.

Chapter 4

Object Oriented Programming Concepts

93: What is an Object in software and what are the benefits of Objects?

Answer:

Software objects consist of state and their behaviour. State of an object is stored in its fields and the behaviour is exposed through the methods. Object oriented programming helps to hide the internal characteristics of an object and this is called encapsulation.

The main advantages of Objects are:

    a) **Independent** – An Object's definition can be kept separate from other objects and passed on to other programs.

    b) **Encapsulation** – The objects fields and characteristics are hidden from the outer world. The only way to access the

c) object's characteristics are through the methods they provide. So the programmer can decide what to hide and what to expose.

d) **Reuse Code**- Existing objects can be reused in many programs by creating an instance or extending its functionality.

e) **Easy to debug** – problematic objects can be traced out and debugged easily without affecting or touching any other portion of the code.

94: Explain method overloading and method overriding
Answer:

Method overloading is when the same method is declared more than once with different arguments. The method name is same but is defined separately for different types or number of arguments. Method overriding is when the same method with the same argument in a super class has a different functionality in the inherited class.

95: Explain interface and inheritance.
Answer:

Inheritance is the method by which the common attributes of a parent class is accessed by a child class which may or may not have additional attributes.

Interface is like a template that defines the basic behaviour of the particular object. How it behaves is defined by the class that inherits the interface. It is much like a parent class with the basic structure.

96: What is a singleton class?

Answer:

A class which lets you create only one instance at any given time is termed a Singleton class. A private constructor with a getter method that returns an object of the same class is used to create singleton class. The getter method will create an object if the object is null.

Example:

```
public class TrialSingleTon {
    private static TrialSingleTon myObj;
        private TrialSingleTon(){
        }
    public static TrialSingleTon getInstance(){
        if(myObj == null){
            myObj = new TrialSingleTon(); // create the object only
            if it is null

        }
        return myObj;
    }
    public void getSomeThing(){
        System.out.println("I am here...");
    }
    public static void main(String a[]){
        TrialSingleTon st = TrialSingleTon.getInstance();
        st.getSomeThing();
    }
}
```

97: State the benefits of Object Orientation.

Answer:

The important benefits of Object Orientation are:

a) **Flexibility**: The code is accessible from anywhere

b) **Extensibility**: The objects used in one class is accessible from another class

c) **Maintainability**: Modifying the code logic requires less time

d) **Reusable code**: The code written in one application is reusable in another application.

98: What do you have to do to implement "flexible", "extensible", and "maintainable" code? Give an example.

Answer:

In order to implement the above features, we have to use the encapsulation concept. It can be implemented by following the three rules given below:

a) The instance variable must always be declared as either private or protected.

b) The method must always be declared as public and these public methods are invoked to access the values of the instance variables.

c) The Java Bean methods declared in a class has to be declared by following the JavaBean naming convention.

For example:

public String getName() { return name;} //Line 1

public void setName(String strName) { this.name = strName;} //Line 2

In Line 1 and Line 2, the method getName and setName denotes the instance variable 'name'.

99: Write a code snippet that uses encapsulation concept.

Answer:

The following code snippet uses encapsulation concept:

```
public class Laptop {
        private String memory;
        public String getMemory() {
                return memory;
        }
        public String setMemory(String newMemory) {
                memory = newMemory;
        }
}
```

100: What are the benefits of inheritance?

Answer:

There are two benefits of inheritance. They are:

a) We can write reusable code.

For example: If we have a method displayPrice() in a super class then this method displayPrice() can be reusable in all its subclasses.

b) We can have many forms (polymorphism)

For example: Assume that we have a method createShape() in super class. We can use the createShape() method in Rectangle subclass and create a rectangle shape. We can also use the createShape() method in Square subclass and create a Square shape.

101: Write a code that uses inheritance concept.

Answer:

Below is the piece of code which uses inheritance concept:

```
class Electronics {
    public void displayPrice() { //Line 1
        System.out.println("Price is ...");
    }
}
class Camera extends Electronics {
    public void displayBatteryDuration() {
        System.out.println("Battery can withstand upto ... hours");
    }
}
public class TestElectronics {
    public static void main(String argument[]) {
        Camera c = new Camera();
        c.displayPrice(); //Line 2
        c.displayBatteryDuration();
    }
}
```

In the above code, we have displayPrice() method (Line 1) declared in super class 'Electronics' which is invoked from the subclass object c (Line 2). This describes the inheritance concept of reusability.

102: What are the types of inheritance relationships?

Answer:

There are two types of inheritance relationships. They are:

a) **IS-A**

Assume that, Camera is a subclass and Electronics is a super class. In that case, we can say that, Camera IS-A an Electronic product.

b) **HAS-A**

Assume that, inside the Camera class, there is an Object called Battery. In that case, we can say that Camera HAS-A object called Battery.

103: Write a piece of code that implements inheritance relationship.

Answer:

Below is the code snippet that implements inheritance IS-A and HAS-A relationship.

```
class Electronics { }
class Camera extends Electronics {
        private Battery myBattery;
}
```

In the above code, Camera IS-A Electronic product.

Camera HAS-A battery.

104: Which is non-polymorphic in Java? State the reasons.

Answer:

Java's runtime class "Object" is considered as non-polymorphic. The reason is that Object is the root of all the classes that exist in Java. So, it is not possible to assign the reference of Object class to other objects.

105: What is the benefit of reference variable? Give an example.

Answer:

The reference variable is mainly used to invoke the properties and methods of a particular class. In other words, it is mainly used to access the objects of a particular class.

For example:

Camera myCamera;

Here, myCamera is a reference variable through which we can access the Camera objects.

106: When we cannot reassign the reference variable to other objects?

Answer:

If we declare the reference as final, then it is not possible to reassign the reference variable to other objects.

For example:

```
final int iValue = 1000;
public void myMethod(int iNumber) {
        iNumber = iValue++; //Line 1
}
```

In the above code, Line 1 is illegal. Because it is not possible to modify the final variable value and reassign that value to other objects.

107: Is it possible to extend more than one class? State the reasons.

Answer:

It is not possible to extend more than one class. This feature is called as multiple inheritance. Java does not support multiple inheritance as considering or using this might become messy. For example, the below piece of code is illegal and will not compile.

  class MySubClass extends MyParentClass, MySuperClass

In the above code, we have extended two classes MyParentClass and MySuperClass which is not allowed in Java. This is because; extending multiple classes is difficult for developers and the code will look messy as it will be difficult to follow the code. So, this feature is not supported using extends keyword.

But multiple inheritance is supported with the help of an interface. We can use an interface in a class with the help of implements keyword.

For example: The interface 'Digital' can be used in 'Camera' class as below:

  class Camera extends Electronics implements Digital

Using interface will be much easier because interface has pre-defined methods and we just need to override those methods if we implement an interface in the class.

108: How will you assign a reference variable to more than one object?

Answer:

Below is the code snippet where a reference variable "refVariable" is assigned to more than one object.

```
class Electronics {
        public void displayPrice() {
```

```
                System.out.println("Display Price");
        }
}
interface Digital {
        public void displayTime();
}
class Camera extends Electronics implements Digital {
        public void displayBatteryDuration() {
                System.out.println("Display Duration");
        }
        public void displayTime() {
                System.out.println("Display Time");
        }
}
public class Test {
        Camera refVariable = new Camera();
        Object object = refVariable;
        Electronics electronics = refVariable;
        Digital digital = refVariable;
}
```

In the above code, Camera is a sub class of Electronics. So, we can create a reference of Camera 'refVariable' and assign that reference 'refVariable' either to the Super Class Object or to the parent class Electronics.

109: How will you differentiate "overloading" and "overriding"?
Answer:

In case of "overloading", we will use the same name of the method that belongs to a particular class but with different arguments.

For example:

```
class MyClass {
        public void myMethod(int intNumber,
        String strValue) {}
        public void myMethod(boolean isTrue, char cValue) {}
}
```

In the above code, we have the same name of the method myMethod in the class 'MyClass' but with different arguments. This is called overloading.

In case of "overriding", we will use the method of super class in sub class with the same type of argument.

For example:

```
class MyParentClass {
        MyParentClass(int iNumber) {}
}
class MySubClass extends MyParentClass {
        MyParentClass(int iValue) {}
}
```

In the above code, the parent class constructor MyParentClass is used in sub class with the same type of argument. This is called overriding.

110: Write a Java code that does method overriding.

Answer:

Below is the Java code where methods are overridden:

```
class Electronics {
    public void charge() {
        System.out.println("All Electronics product has to be
        charged");
    }
}
class Camera extends Electronics {
    public void charge() {
        System.out.println("The Camera has to be charged
        periodically");
    }
}
```

In the above code, "Camera" subclass overrides the charge() method of "Electronics" super class.

111: Write a Java code that does method overloading.

Answer:

Below is the Java code where methods are overloaded:

```
class Laptop {
    public void displayPixel(int width, int height) { }; //Line 1
    public void displayPixel(float width, float height) {}; //Line 2
}
```

In the above code, in Line 1, displayPixel method has two arguments of type int and int. In Line 2, displayPixel method has two arguments of type float and float. This concept of using same method name but different type of arguments in a class is called method overloading.

112: Find the below code.

class Electronics {

    public void displayPrice(Float price) {} //Line 1

}

class Camera extends Electronics {

    public void displayPrice(String price) {} //Line 2

}

What will happen if you compile and execute the above code? Also state if it uses overloaded or overridden method?

Answer:

The above code will compile fine. It has used method overloading because the method names are same but arguments are different. In Line 1, the argument type for method displayPrice() is Float. In Line 2, the argument type for method displayPrice() is String. This concept is called method overloading.

113: Give examples for illegal method overrides.

Answer:

Below code snippet is an illegal method override:

    class Electronics {

        public void displayPrice() {}

    }

    class Camera extends Electronics {

        public void displayPrice() throws Exception {}

    }

114: How will you define a constructor? Give an example.

Answer:

Constructor is a special method which has the same name as the class name but with no return type. These methods are invoked automatically by the Java Virtual Machine (JVM) whenever it executes the Line1 from the main method as explained below.

For example:

```
class Electronics {
        Electronics() {}
        public static void main(String argument[]) {
                Electronics e = new Electronics(); //Line 1
        }
}
```

In the above code, the constructor Electronics() has no return type and is invoked when Line 1 is executed by JVM.

115: What is the use of constructors?

Answer:

The constructors are mainly used to initialize the value for the instance variable. It is also used to invoke the super class constructor using the super() keyword.

For example:

```
        class Camera extends Electronics {
                String cameraName;
                Camera() {
                        super(); //Line 1
                        cameraName = "SLR - XYZ" // Line 2
                }
                Camera (String cameraName) {
                        this. cameraName = cameraName;
```

        }
    }

In the above code, in Line 2, the instance variable 'cameraName' is initialized inside the constructor and in Line 1, we have used super() to invoke the super class (Electronics) constructor.

116: Have a look at the below code:
class Laptop {
        Laptop(String laptopName) {
                System.out.println("Laptop Name is ...");
        }
        public static void main(String argument[]) {
                Laptop l = new Laptop();
        }
}

What will be the output when we compile and execute the above code?

Answer:

The code will not compile and it will throw the below compilation error:

        "The constructor Laptop() is undefined."

We need to define a empty constructor Laptop() {} in order for the program to get compiled.

117: What is the use of super() and where to use this?

Answer:

super() is mainly used to call or invoke the constructor or method of the super class or parent class from the sub class. We have to

declare super() in the first line of the subclass's constructor.
For example:

```
class Electronics {
        Electronics() {} // Line 1
}
class Camera extends Electronics {
        String cameraName;
        Camera() {
                super(); //Line 2
                cameraName = "SLR - XYZ" // Line 2
        }
}
```

In the above code, Line 1 is invoked with the use of super() which is defined in Line 2.

118: Have a look at the below code:
```
class Employee {
        Employee getName(String name) {
                return new Employee();
        }
}
```
What happens when you compile the above code? What is the return type called?

Answer:

The code gets compiled without any error. This type of return type is called as covariant returns. This type is supported from 1.5 version and if this is compiled in 1.4, it throws compiler error "incompatible return type".

119: What are the possible access modifiers for a constructor?

Answer:

Below are the possible access modifiers for a constructor:

a) **private**: This denotes that the constructor is accessible only from its class

b) **public**: This denotes that the constructor is accessible from any class which resides in any package

c) **protected**: This denotes that the constructor is accessible from any class which resides in the same package

120: What happens behind the scenes if you do not include a constructor in the class?

Answer:

If we do not include a constructor in the class, the compiler will automatically generate a default constructor. The default constructor is a no argument constructor which is created by the Java Virtual Machine, only in the case that, there are no other constructors available in the particular class.

121: Have a look at the below code:

```
class Electronics {
        Electronics() {}
        public void displayPrice() {
                Electronics();
        }
}
```

What happens when you compile the above code?

Answer:

On compiling the above code, it gives compilation error "The method Electronics() is undefined for the type Electronics.". It is always illegal to call a constructor because the constructor is invoked by the Java Virtual Machine by default.

Chapter 5

Declarations and Access Controls

122: You are given an assignment to create a game of Tic Tac Toe using a multi dimensional array. How do you initialize the array?

    a) int ttt   =new int[3][3];

    b) int[]ttt   =new int[3][3];

    c) int[][]ttt =new int[3][3];

    d) int ttt [3][3]=new int[][];

Answer:

(c) is correct. The correct syntax for declaring a multi-dimensional array is

    int[][]ttt =new int[3][3];

123: Examine the code given below and explain the result when you compile it.

```
public class ArrayDec {
    public static void main(String argv[]){
        ArrayDec ad = new ArrayDec ();
        ad.arrayMethod();
    }
    public void arrayMethod (){
        int intArr1[]= {1,2,3};
        int[] intArr2 = {1,2,3};
        int  intArr3[] = new int[] {1,2,3};
        System.out.print(intArr3.length);
    }
}
```

    a)   **Compilation and output of 3**

    b)   **Compilation but no output**

    c)   **Compile time error, arrays do not have a length field**

    d)   **Compile time error, intArr3 is not created correctly**

Answer:

a) The program compiles and produces the output 3.

Since all of the array declarations are correct, the program will compile and print the output as 3 which is intArray3's length.

124: What is the benefit of declaring a class as final?

Answer:

By declaring a class as final, we ensure that the class is secured thereby no one can change its existing implementation. Also, the final class is thread-safe thereby restricting interaction between multiple threads.

For example:

    final class MyClass {}

By making the class 'MyClass' as final, it is not possible for us to extend this class and use its implementation. Also, inter-thread communication is not possible when we declare the class as final.

125: How will you define an Identifier?

Answer:

Identifiers are defined as the naming conventions which are used to define a class, variable, method or interface. Identifiers must start with an alphabet, a currency character ($), or a connecting character such as _.

Some of the examples of legal identifiers are shown below:

_b

$a

___1_c

_$

This_is_a_valid_identifier

126: What are access and non-access modifiers? Give examples.

Answer:

Modifiers are keywords which restrict or allow access to a class, method, or variable you create. It provides visibility for people trying to access from within or outside of a particular class.

The Java access modifiers are public, private, protected, and default.

If a class is declared as 'public' the class is visible to all the classes from all the packages.

If a class is declared as 'private' the class is not visible to other classes.

If a class is declared as 'protected' the class is visible to its package and other packages except subclasses.

If a class is not declared with an access modifier, then it is considered as 'default' and it is accessible to all classes in the same package. For example: class Test

In the above line, Test class is not declared with an access modifier and so it has default access modifier.

The non-access Java modifiers are static, abstract, final, and strictfp.

Each of the non-access modifiers are keywords which serve a different purpose as described below.

If a class is declared as 'static' this class will be executed first.

If a class is declared as 'abstract' the class cannot be instantiated.

If a class is declared as 'final' the class cannot be subclassed.

If a class is declared as 'strictfp' then it means that all the methods declared in that particular class confirm to IEEE 754 standard rules for floating points.

127: How will you declare a compilable abstract class?
Answer:

A compilable abstract class can be declared as below.

public abstract class Parrot {

            public Sound speak() {}

}

An Abstract class will always be declared with an "abstract" keyword. The methods declared in an abstract class may or may not have abstract methods.

128: How will you declare a method name that follows JavaBean standard?

Answer:

The JavaBean standard follows camel case notation where the first letter of first word starts with a small letter and the first letter of the second word starts with a capital letter.

Examples of declaring a method name that follows JavaBean standards are given below:

    a)   void invokeMethod() {}

    b)   public void callName() {}

    c)   String doThings() {return null;}

    d)   Void goFast() {}

129: What is the main purpose of Garbage Collection?

Answer:

The main purpose of Garbage Collection is to delete any unwanted objects that are available in the memory. Garbage collection provides automated memory management feature which is handled by the JVM (Java Virtual Machine) during run time. The JVM removes all the objects that are no longer required and clears the memory.

130: How will you declare the 'MyInterface' interface in an abstract class 'MyAbstract'?

Answer:

The interface 'MyInterface' can be declared in the abstract class 'MyAbstract' as below:

abstract class MyAbstract implements MyInterface {

}

An interface is always declared with the help of "implements" keyword. It is not really required to overwrite the methods of an interface when we implement the interface from an abstract class.

131: What are the possible ways of declaring compilable Java main method?

Answer:

Following are the possible ways of declaring compilable Java main method.

    a) public static void main (String argument[])
    b) static public void main(String argument[])

132: What are the possible ways of declaring compilable short type array?

Answer:

Following are the possible ways of declaring compilable short type array.

    a) short a1 [];
    b) short [] b1;
    c) short [] c1 [] [];

133: What are the possible ways of declaring compilable Java class?

Answer:

Following are the possibile ways of declaring compilable Java class.

a) public class Class1 {}

b) class Class2 {}

c) private class Class3 {}

d) protected class Class4 {}

134: An interface and its method is described as below:

interface MyInterface {

    int myValue = 1;

    void invoke();

}

How will the compiler consider the interface's constant and method's access control?

Answer:

The above interface constant is implicitly considered as public, static, and final. The interface method invoke() is implicitly considered as public and abstract.

135: What are the possible ways of declaring compilable interface?

Answer:

Following are the possible ways of declaring compilable interface:

a) interface Interface1 {}

b) public interface Interface2 {}

   c)   public abstract interface Interface3 {}

   d)   abstract interface Interface4 {}

   e)   abstract public interface Interface5 {}

136: What are the various types of primitive variables?

Answer:

There are eight types of primitive variables. They are

   a)   **byte**: It holds value from -128 to 128 (8 bit)

   b)   **short**: It holds value from -32768 to 32767 (16 bit)

   c)   **char**: It holds value from 0 to 65535 (16 bit)

   d)   **Boolean**: It can hold either 'true' or 'false'

   e)   **int**: It holds value from -2,147,483,648 to 2,147,483,647 (32 bit)

   f)   **long**: It holds value from -9,223,372,036,854,775,808 to 9,223,372,036,854,775,807 (64 bit)

   g)   **float**: It is a single precision 32-bit floating point

   h)   **double**: It is a 64-bit double precision floating point

137: How does reference variable differ from primitive variable?

Answer:

The primitive variable is used to assign a value to the variable.

For example:

     int iValue = 1000;

The reference variables are used to refer any object in order to access the objects.

For example:

     ParentClass p = new ParentClass();

     p.invokeMethod();

138: Assume that class Test contains the following piece of code:

static void main(String argument[]) {

      System.out.println("This gets printed");

}

What will be the output if you try to compile and run this piece of code?

Answer:

The above piece of code will compile fine. But on executing, the JVM (Java Virtual Machine) launcher will throw the run time error saying "Main method not public."

139: Assume that there exists the following classes and method:

package com.questions;

public class CoreJava {

      private String getQuestion() {

            return "Question1";

      }

}

package com.questions;

class JSP extends CoreJava {

      public void getJSPQuestion() {

            Sytem.out.println(getQuestion());

      }

}

What will happen when you try to compile and run the above code?

Answer:

The above code will not compile because the private method

getQuestion() is not visible to getJSPQuestion() method. The rule is that a private method cannot be overridden by a subclass.

140: What is the best practice in declaring instance variables?

Answer:

The instance variable always has to be declared as private and protected. This is a way to protect the instance variable so that the value gets modified under the programmer's control. We can always declare an instance variable as public. But it is not advisable to do so.

141: Assume that we have the following piece of code:

```
public abstract class Machine {
        private ArrayList list;
        public abstract void getMachineList();
        public ArrayList getList() {
                return list;
        }
}
```

What happens when you compile and execute the above code? State the reasons.

Answer:

The above code will compile just fine, because an abstract class can have both abstract and non-abstract methods.

142: Can an instance variable be declared as static? State the reasons.

Answer:

An instance variable cannot be declared as static. If we declare an instance variable as static, then that variable will become a class variable.

143: What are the modifiers that should not be used for declaring the instance variable?

Answer:

We should not use the following modifiers while declaring an instance variable:

a) Abstract

b) synchronized

c) native

d) strictfp

Since it is not possible to create a reference to the abstract class, creating an instance variable in an abstract class cannot be utilized. So, abstract modifier is not supported to declare instance variable.

The other modifiers synchronized, native and strictfp are used only with method declaration and not valid for declaring instance variables.

144: What are the modifiers that can be used while declaring a method?

Answer:

Following are the modifiers that can be used while declaring a method:

a) public

b) private

c) protected

d) static

e) final

f) abstract

g) native

h) synchronized

i) strictfp

All of the above modifiers are supported in Java by default to access objects either from a single application or from multiple applications.

145: How will you define the types of variables?

Answer:

The variables can be defined in two types. They are

a) **Primitive variable:** This is used to store different types of values like integer, boolean, char, long, float, double, char, byte, and short

b) **Reference variable:** This is used to store objects

146: What is the benefit of using the keyboards "transient" and "native"?

Answer:

The keyword "transient" is used with non-local variable as a modifier and the keyword "native" is used as a modifier with methods.

By making the variable as transient, we are instructing JVM to ignore the variable when you attempt to serialize the containing object.

By making method as native, the method can be implemented in another platform independent language such as C.

147: Is "volatile" a keyword? If so, where will you use it?

Answer:

Yes, "volatile" is a keyword mainly used with non-local variable as a modifier. It is mainly used if multiple threads need to communicate with one another. By using volatile modifier, the variable is thread-safe and it provides the possibility of inter thread communication.

148: What are the modifiers that can be used while declaring a non-local variable?

Answer:

Following are the modifiers that can be used while declaring a non-local variable:

   a) private
   b) public
   c) protected
   d) static
   e) final
   f) transient
   g) volatile

The above modifiers are used to make the variables accessible from a particular class or from different classes.

This page is intentionally left blank.

Chapter 6

Java Assignments

149: Given the following variables, which of the following assignments will compile without error?

String str = "Hello";

long lng = 99;

double dbl = 1.11;

int i = 1;

int j = 0;

    a) j = i << str;

    b) j = i << j;

    c) j = i << dbl;

    d) j = i << lng;

Answer:

The 2nd and 4th assignments will compile without any error.

    a) j = i << j;

    b) j = i << lng;

You cannot use assign operators with incompatible primitives. int and string are not compatible. Similarly int and double are not compatible.

150: What will be the output of the following set of statements?

```
Int x = -1;
x = x>>>24;
System.out.println(x);
```

    a) 0

    b) -1

    c) 1

    d) 255

Answer:

d) 255

Here, x is set to –1, which will set all 32 bits to 1 converting into binary. The value is then shifted right by 24 bits, filling the first 24 bits with 0s, not considering the sign extension. This sets x to 255.

11111111 11111111 11111111 11111111 represents -1 in binary

>>>24

00000000 00000000 00000000 00000000 is the binary version of 255

151: Examine the following code and explain what happens when you run it.

```
Public class Trial{
    public static void main(String argv[]){
        int x, y, z = 2;
        System.out.println( x * y | z);
    }
```

}

    a) **Compiles and gives output of 4**

    b) **Compiles and gives output of 6**

    c) **Compiles and gives output of 2**

    d) **Gives compile time errors - operators cannot be sequenced in this mode**

Answer:

The answer is a). The program compiles and gives the output 4. The * operator has a higher priority than the | operator. Thus the computation is equal to (2 * 2) | 2 or you can consider it 4 * 2. The | operator evaluates the bits in each place and if a bit is there in a place in either number then the output figure also has a bit in that position. 100 is the bit value for 4 and the bit sequence for 10 for 2. The outcome of the | process will be 110 which is equal to 6 decimal.

152: Which of the following are valid statements?

    a) **System.out.println(2+2);**

    b) **int i= 2+'2';**

    c) **String s= "two"+'two';**

    d) **byte b=256;**

Answer:

The valid statements are :

    a) System.out.println(2+2);

    b) int i= 2+'2';

Option c) is not valid since single quotes are used to point to a character constant and not a string.

Option d) will not compile since 256 is out of the range of a byte.

153: What gets printed on the standard output when the class below is compiled and executed?

```
public class ShortCkt {
    public static void main(String abc[]) {
        int i = 0;
        boolean abc = true;
        boolean efg = false, xyz;
        xyz = (abc & ((valNo++) == 0));
        xyz = (efg & ((valNo +=2) > 0));
        System.out.println(valNo);
    }
}
```

Answer:

The output is 3. First valNo ++ will increase the value of valNo by 1 and make it 1. Then valNo +=2 will increase valNo by 2 making valNo = 3. So System.out.println(valNo) will print 3.

154: What is Heap and Stack?

Answer:

Heap is a memory region that exists in the computer operating system in which Java objects are allocated or freed dynamically. All the instance variables and objects declared in Java will be stored in heap. The objects stored in heap exist for a longer duration and the objects are removed automatically if they are not used.

Stack is another memory region in the computer operating system where the Java objects are allocated in LIFO (Last In First Out) concept. All the method and local variables declared in Java will be stored in stack. The objects stored in stack exist for a short duration and the objects are automatically removed if not used.

155: Look at the below code:

```
class Electronics { }
class Camera {
        Electronics e;
        String cameraName;
        public static void main(String argument[]) {
                Camera c = new Camera();
                c.getPrice(c);
        }
        public void getPrice(Camera camera) {
                e = new Electronics();
        }
}
```

From the above code, what gets into heap and what gets into stack?

Answer:

All the instance variables and its objects get into heap. The instance variables and objects that are stored in heap (from the above code) are "cameraName", "e", "Electronics", and "Camera".

All the methods and its local variables get into stack. The method and its local variables that are stored in stack (from the above code) are "main()", "getPrice()", "c", and "camera".

156: What is a string literal? Give an example.

Answer:

A string literal is a value assigned to the String object. It is assigned to the String object with the help of an assignment operator (=). The following line of code shows that the string literal "I'm a literal" is assigned to the string object 'name'.

    String name = "I'm a literal";

157: How will you cast an "int" literal to "byte" explicitly? Is it really necessary to cast "int" literal to "byte"?

Answer:

The "int" literal can be cast to "byte" as below:

    byte bValue = (byte) 30;

It is not really necessary to cast "int" literal to "byte". By default, the compiler takes care of casting "int" literal to "byte".

158: Give an example for implicit cast.

Answer:

The below line of code is an example for implicit cast:

    int iValue = 250;

    long lValue = iValue;

The above code explains that an int value can always be assigned to a long variable without casting and the conversion happens by default.

159: Write two lines of code using casting and explain how will you assign a "float" to a "short"?

Answer:

Below are the two lines of code through which we can assign a "float" to a "short" using casting:

> float fValue = 37000.02F;
>
> short sValue = (short) fValue;

160: What are the possible ways to assign a "float" literal to a "float" variable?

Answer:

Below are the possible ways to assign a "float" literal to a "float" variable:

> float fValue1 = 100.5f;
>
> float fValue2 = 100.5F;
>
> float fValue3 = (float) 100.5;

The float literal is always followed with 'f' or 'F'. If the float literal does not have 'f' or 'F', then it should be cast as a float type before declaring the value.

161: Look at the below code:

byte bValue = 10;

bValue = bValue + 10;

Will the above code get compiled? If not, what will you do to make it compile?

Answer:

The above code will not compile as the result will be an "int". So, in order for that to compile, we can use any of the below lines of code:

> bValue += 10;
>
> bValue = (byte) (bValue + 10);

162: Look at the below code:

```
class Electronics {
        public void displayPrice() {}
}
class Camera extends Electronics {
        public void displayname() {}
}
class TestElectronics {
        public static void main(String argument[]) {
                Electronics e = new Camera(); //Line 1
                Camera c = new Electronics(); //Line 2
        }
}
```

Have a look at line 1 and line 2. Which line will compile and which will not?

Answer:

Line 1 compiles fine and Line 2 will not compile. The reason is: We can always assign a subclass to its parent class but not the parent class to a subclass of the declared type. This is because the child object is derived from the parent object but the parent object is not derived from child object.

163: How will you define scope and what are the different types of scope in variables?

Answer:

Scope often refers to how the variable can be accessed and how long it exists.

There are four basic scopes which exist for a specific period of time as shown below:

a) The longest scope exists for static variables. It exists until the class remains in JVM.

b) The next most lived scope exists for instance variables. Until you remove the instance, the scope exists.

c) The next one is local variables. Until the method exists in the stack, the scope exists.

d) The next one is Block variables. The scope exists until the code block is executed.

164: How will you define an Octal and Hexadecimal literal in an "int" variable?

Answer:

The Octal and Hexadecimal literal can be defined in an "int" variable as below:

```
int iValue1 = 0100;
int iValue2 = 0xf1dead;
```

The Octal literal is prefixed with '0' before assigning the value. The octal values are in the range of 0-7

The Hexadecimal literal is prefixed with '0x' before assigning the value. The hexadecimal values are in the range of 0-9 and may contain A, B, C, D, E, and F.

165: What are the possible ways of declaring a "double" literal in a "double" variable?

Answer:

Following are the possible ways of declaring a "double" literal in a "double" variable:

```
double dValue1 = 100.199;
double dValue2 = 100.199d;
double dValue3 = 100.199D;
```

The double literal is assigned with the character 'd' or 'D' or even without the character.

166: Look at the below code:

```
char cValue1 = '@'; //Line 1
char CValue2 = '\u004E'; //Line 2
char cValue3 = 80000; //Line 3
char cValue4 = (char) -100; //Line 4
char cValue5 = 128; //Line 5
```

Which line will compile and which will not?

Answer:

Except Line 3, all lines will compile because the range of character is from 0 to 65,536. In order for the line 3 to compile we have to modify the line as below:

```
char cValue3 = (char) 80000;
```

167: What is the default value for "Boolean" and "char" type instance variable?

Answer:

The default value for "Boolean" type instance variable is false.
The default value for "char" type instance variable is '\u0000'.

168: What will be the default value of a reference variable when it is not explicitly initialized? How will you handle this in code?

Answer:

When the reference variable is not explicitly initialized, then it is value will be null by default. In order to handle this situation in code, we have to check if the object is not null and execute the reference steps.

169: Look at the below code:

```
public class Test {
        public static void main(String argument[]) {
                int iValue;
                System.out.println(iValue);
        }
}
```

What will happen when you compile and execute the above code?

Answer:

The code will not compile because the local variable is not initialized. So, a local variable also called as an automatic variable must be initialized with a value.

170: What is the default value for "float", "double", "byte", "short", "int", and "long" type instance varibles?

Answer:

The default value for "float" and "double" type instance variable is 0.0.

The default value for "byte", "short", "int", and "long" type instance variable is 0.

171: Have a look at the below code:

```
class Calculate {
        float fValue = 10.2f;
        public static void main(String argument[]) {
                System.out.println("Float value is: "+fValue);
        }
}
```

What will happen when the above code is executed?

Answer:

The above code will not get compiled because we are trying to access a non-static instance variable from a static method which is not possible.

172: How will you declare a "primitive array" and "reference array"?

Answer:

The "primitive array" can be declared as below:

a)   int [] iArray1;

b)   int iArray2 [];

The "reference array" can be declared as below:

a)   String [] strArray1;

b)   String [] strArray2 [];

c)   String [][][] strArray3;

It is not recommended to follow the ii) approach.

173: Have a look at the below code:

int [] [] add = new int [2] []; //Line 1

int [] subtract = new int [2]; //Line 2

int iValue = 2; //Line 3

add[1] = subtract; //Line 4

add[1] = iValue; //Line 5

From the above code, which line gets compiled and which line does not?

Answer:

In the above code, all lines get compiled except Line 5 because we cannot assign an int variable to an int array variable.

174: Have a look at the below code:

```
public class Test {
  public static void main(string argument[]) {
    int iValue = 100;
    Test test = new Test();
    System.out.println("The value before modification: "+iValue);
    test.invokeMethod(iValue);
    System.out.println("The value after modification: "+iValue);
  }
  public void invokeMethod(int iValue2) {
    iValue2 = iValue2 + 100;
    System.out.println("iValue2 is : "+iValue2);
  }
}
```

What will be the output for the above code?

Answer:

When we compile and execute the above code, we will get the below output:

The value before modification: 100

iValue2 is : 200

The value after modification: 100

175: What are the possible ways of declaring int array literal to an int array variable?

Answer:

Following are the possible ways of declaring an int array literal to an int array variable:

    a)   int [] iArray1 = {1, 2, 3, 4, 5};

    b)   int [] iArray2;

iArray2 = new int[5];

iArray2[0] = 1;

iArray2[1] = 2;

iArray2[2] = 3;

iArray2[3] = 4;

iArray2[4] = 5;

176: Have a look at the below code:

```
class Test {
  public static void main(String argument[]) {
   Test test = new Test();
   System.out.println("iValue: "+iValue);
   invokeMethod(iValue);
   System.out.println("iValue after invocation is: "+iValue);
  }
  static int iValue = 100;
  static void invokeMethod(int iValue) {
    iValue = iValue + 100;
    System.out.println("iValue in invokeMethod is: "+iValue);
```

}

}

What will be the output for the above code?

Answer:

When we compile and execute the above code, following will be the output:

iValue: 100

iValue in invokeMethod is: 200

iValue after invocation is: 100

177: Look at the below code:

```
public class Car {
        public Car(String carName) {}
}
Car myCar = new Car("Benz");
Car [] myCars = { myCar, new Car("Ford"), new Car("BMW")};
```
What happens when we compile the above code? State the reasons.

Answer:

The code compiles fine and there is no issue at all. In the above code, "Car" array is referenced by the variable "myCar" which has three values (Benz, Ford, BMW) in it.

178: What happens when we compile and execute the below code?

```
int [] iArray = new int[5];
int iInt = -5;
iArray[iInt] = 5;
```

Answer:

The code compiles fine but it will throw the RunTimeException "ArrayIndexOutofBoundsException", because iInt is a negative number which cannot be assigned as an array position.

Chapter 7

Java Operators

179: What type of value does an instanceOf operator return?

Answer:

The instanceOf operator returns a Boolean value. If both the objects being compared are of same type it will return true and otherwise it will return false.

180: What will be the output for System.out.println(3 + 5 * 9 / 3);?

Answer:

The result will be 18 because the precedence of * & / are greater and it will be processed from left to right. So first 9/3 is processed which is 3, then 5*3 which is 15 and then 3+15 which is 18.

181: What are the types of relational operators in Java?

Answer:

There are four types of relational operators in Java. They are:

a) >

This is called as 'Greater Than' operator

b) >=

This is called as 'Greater Than Equal To' operator

c) <

This is called as 'Less Than' operator

d) <=

This is called as 'Less Than Equal To' operator.

182: What are the logical operators in Java?

Answer:

There are six types of logical operators in Java. They are:

a) &

b) |

c) ^

d) !

e) &&

f) ||

The operators &, |, ^ are called as Bitwise operators.

The operator ! is called as boolean invert.

The operators && , || are called as short-circuit operators.

The operators &, | are also called as non-short circuit operators.

183: What are called as Arithmetic operators?

Answer:

The following are called as the Arithmetic operators:

a) + (This is a plus operator used to add numbers)

b) − (This is a minus operator used to subtract numbers)

c) * (This is a multiplication operator used to multiply numbers)

d) / (This is a division operator used to divide numbers)

184: Which operators are used for String concatenation and how will you concatenate a String? Give an example.

Answer:

The operator + is used for String concatenation. A String can be concatenated as shown below:

String sum = "one" + "two";

In the above code, the values one and two are concatenated and assigned to a String object "sum".

185: What will be the output of the below code?

```
public class Test {
        public static void main (String argument[]) {
                String name = "Java";
                int iInt1 = 100;
                int iInt2 = 200;
                System.out.println( name + iInt1 + iInt2);
        }
}
```

Answer:

The above code compiles fine and it gives the below output:

Java100200

Since + operator is used with a String variable and int variable, the final value is considered as a String and the values are concatenated and displayed.

186: State the name of % operator and explain how will you use this?

Answer:

The % operator is called as modulus or remainder operator.

This operator always returns the remainder of a particular value.

For example:

The value of 100 % 4 is 0.

The value of 10 % 4 is 2.

When we divide 4 from 100, the remainder is 0 and when we divide 4 from 10, the remainder is 2.

187: Have a look at the below lines of code:

int ivalue = 100;

System.out.println(ivalue + 100); //Line 1

System.out.println(ivalue + "" + 100); //Line 2

Will the code compile? If so, what will be the output for Line 1 and Line 2?

Answer:

The code compiles fine and the output of Line 1 and Line 2 is 200 and 100100 respectively. If we try to add an empty string, JVM assumes that it is String concatenation and displays the output accordingly.

188: Which are the two relational operators that are called as equality operators? Give an example.

Answer:

The relational operators == and != are called as equality operators. These operators are used to compare two values which will return a boolean value (either true or false) as shown below.

For example:

```
int iValue = 10;
if(iValue == 10) {// Line 1
  if(iValue != 10) {//Line 2
    System.out.println("This will not be printed");
  }
}
```

In the above code, Line 1 returns true and the statements below "if" will be executed. So, Line 2 is executed. Since Line 2 returns false the statements below that "if" block will not be executed.

189: Will the below lines of code compile? If so, what will be the output?

```
boolean b1 = ('x' == 'x'); //Line 1
boolean b2 = ('x' == 'y'); //Line 2
boolean b3 = (100.0 == 100L); //Line 3
System.out.println("b1: "+ b1 +"\nb2: "+ b2 + "\nb3: "+b3); //Line 4
```

Answer:

All the above lines (Line 1, Line 2, Line 3, and Line 4) are legal and will compile fine. The output will be displayed as:

> b1: true
>
> b2: false
>
> b3: true

In Line 1, we compare the reference of x with x which returns a boolean value true.

In Line 2, we compare the reference of y with x which returns a boolean value false.

In line 3, we compare 2 long values which returns a boolean value true.

190: What happens when we compile the below code? What will be the output?

```
boolean bValue = false;
if(bValue = true) { //Line 1
        System.out.println("The value is "+bValue);
}
else
{
        System.out.println("The value is "+bValue);
}
```

Answer:

The code compiles fine. In the above code, in line 1, we are not using comparison operator ==, just the assignment operator =. We have assigned boolean value to the boolean variable bValue. Since the return type is boolean, the code compiles fine. So, the output will be:

> The value is true

191: How will you represent increment and decrement operators?

Answer:

The increment operators are always represented as two plus signs and the decrement operators are represented as two minus signs. So, the increment and decrement operators are represented as below:

a) ++

b) --

192: What happens when we compile the below code? What will be the output?

```
final int iIntFinal = 100;
int iValue = iIntFinal ++;
System.out.println("The output is: "+iValue);
```

Answer:

The code will not compile and it throws a compiler error as the final variable is using a compound assignment ++ and it is assigned to an int variable. The code will work fine if the final variable is simply assigned to an int variable.

193: What happens when we compile the code mentioned below? What will be the output?

```
int iValue = 100;
if(iValue = 100) {
        System.out.println("iValue is : "+iValue);
}
```

Answer:

The code will not compile and it throws a compilation error. This is because we are assigning an int literal to an int variable and so the return type is int. The return type should always be boolean if we use any statement within if condition.

194: What will be the output when you compile and execute the code mentioned below?

```
int iValue1 = 10;
int iValue2 = 6;
System.out.println( iValue1 + " "+ (iValue1 % iValue2));
```

Answer:

The code compiles just file and displays the below output:

        10 4

Because of the empty String concatenation, the output will display as a String.

195: What is a ternary operator? Give an example.

Answer:

The ternary operator is also called as a conditional operator as it has operands. It is mainly used to evaluate a boolean expression. For example:

```
int iValue1 = 100;
int iValue2 = (iValue1 == 100) ? 200 : 100; //Line 1
```

In the above code, == denotes the conditional operator. The boolean expression 'iValue1 == 100' returns true and so the value 200 will be assigned to the variable iValue2.

196: What will be the value of "a" and "b" when the below code is executed?

```
jnt a = 0;
int b = 0;
for (int c = 0; c < 5 ; c++) {
        if((++a > 2) || (++b >2)) //Line 1
                a++; // Line 2
}
```

Answer:

When the above code is executed, the value of "a" will be 8 and the value of "b" will be 2.

The 'for' loop executes for 4 times and for every execution of Line 1 and Line 2, the value of "a" will be incremented. So, the value of "a" will be 8.

Although 'for' loop executes for 4 times, because of the short circuit operator | |, when the condition ++a is true, the condition ++b > 2 is never checked by the JVM. So the value of b will be 2.

197: State the use of instanceof operator. Give an example.

Answer:

The use of instanceof operator is to check if an object belongs to a particular type. So, it is used only with object reference variables. For example:

```
String name = "This is Java";
if (name instanceof String) {
        System.out.println(name);
}
```

The above code checks if the variable 'name' is of type String. Since the condition is true, it will print the result "This is Java" when you execute the above code.

198: Will the code mentioned below compile? If so, what will be the output?
```
static String callMe() {
        return " This is called";
}
```

```
Long l1 = 10L; Long l2 = 20L;
System.out.println(l1 + l2 + callMe()); //Line 1
```

Answer:

The code compiles fine and the output will be

    30 This is called

When Line 1 is executed from the above code, the expression is executed from left to right. So, the value of l1 is added to l2 which gives 30 and then the String is concatenated with the value 30. So, the value is displayed as "30 This is called".

199: Will the below line of code compile? If so, what will be the value?

```
int [] iArray = new int[10];
if(iArray instanceof Object) { //Line 1
        System.out.println("Object");
}
else
{
        System.out.println("int");
}
```

Answer:

The above code compiles fine and it displays the below result:

    Object

The reason is, when line 1 is executed, the condition returns true. It is because an array is always considered as an object instance.

200: What happens when you execute the below code?

```
Button button1 = new Button("Save");
```

Button button2 = new Button("Save");

Button button3 = button2; // Line 1

if(button1 == button2) { //Line 2

      System.out.println("button1 equals button2");

}

if(button3 == button2) { // Line 3

      System.out.println("button3 equals button 2");

}

Answer:

The code compiles fine and displays the below output:

      button3 equals button2

The reason is, when line 1 is executed, the reference of button2 is assigned to button3 which means that, the bits of button2 are assigned to button3. Because of that, when line 3 is executed the condition becomes true and the output is displayed as above.

201: How will you define "^" operator? What is its use?

Answer:

The "^" is a Bitwise (or) a non-short circuit operator which is also called as XOR (Exclusive-OR). It is mainly used to evaluate boolean values only.

For example:

      byte bValue = 5 ^ 3; //Line 1

The value of 5 is denoted as 0101

The value of 3 is denoted as 0011

XOR returns 0 when both values are 0 or both values are 1 as highlighted below.

```
0 1 0 1
0 0 1 1
----------
0 1 1 0
```

The value of 0110 is 6. So, when line 1 is executed, the value 6 is assigned to the byte variable bValue.

202: What will be the output on executing the code below?

```
int iValue = 10;
int jValue =20;
if(iValue && jValue) {
        System.out.println(True will be printed...");
}
else
{
        System.out.println("False will be printed...");
}
```

Answer:

The above code will not compile because the short circuit operator && is used with int but it will work with boolean operands only.

203: What will be the output of the below line of code? Give explanation.

```
System.out.println("Output is "+ ((10 < 100) ^ (100 > 10)));
```

Answer:

The output will be displayed as

Output is false

The reason is:

10 < 100 returns true which can be denoted as 1

100 > 10 returns true which can be denoted as 1

As per XOR rule, when both values are 1, the result is 0 which can be denoted as false. So, the output is displayed as above.

204: Explain about postfix and prefix operators. Give example.

Answer:

Postfix operator gets executed after assigning the value to an expression.

For example:

> int iValue = 10;
>
> int jValue = iValue + iValue ++; //Line 1
>
> The value of jValue is 20.

When Line 1 is executed, the expression is calculated as int jValue = 10 + 10 because of postfix operator and so the value of 'jValue' becomes 20. Once line 1 gets executed, the postfix operator (iValue++) is executed and iValue becomes 11.

Prefix operator gets executed before assigning the value to an expression.

For example:

> int iValue = 10;
>
> int jValue = iValue + ++iValue ; //Line 2
>
> The value of jValue is 21.

When Line 2 is executed, the expression is calculated as int jValue = 10 + 11 because of the prefix operator and so the value of jValue becomes 21. So, when we use prefix operator (++ivalue), the value is calculated first and then it is added to another value.

205: What will be output of the below lines of code? Give explanation.

```
if(!(100 == 1000)) {
        System.out.println("TRUE gets printed");
}
else
{
        System.out.println("FALSE gets printed");
}
```

Answer:

The output will be displayed as

        TRUE gets printed

The reason is:

  When 100 == 1000 is executed, the value is returned as false.

  When !false is executed, the value is returned as true and so the output is displayed as above.

The NOT operator is also called as boolean invert operator which always returns the opposite value of the current value of boolean.

Chapter 8

Inner Classes and String Handling

206: What is the output? Explain.

```
class tryImmutableString{
    public static void main(String strAgrs[]) {
        String strVar = "Welcome";
        strVar.concat(" to Java");
        System.out.println(strVar);
    }
}
```

Answer:

The output is Welcome. Java strings are immutable objects meaning, unless explicitly assigned, the string's value does not change. If the code was strVar = strVar.concat(" to Java"); then the print would have yielded Welcome to Java. Even when assigned, a new string object is created and assigned the value Welcome to Java and the original value Hello remains the same.

207: What is an inner class? What are the different ways an inner class can be defined?

Answer:

An inner class is any class defined inside the body of another class. An inner class will have access to all members of the outer class. Inner classes can be defined in 4 ways:

a) **Inner class** – New Class is defined within the body of another class. Inner class can access all members of outer class. You can access a nested class by instantiating an object of outer class.

b) **Method** – local inner class – Class is defined inside a method of another class. Here the inner class can access only final members.

c) **Anonymous inner class** – has no name and can be instantiated only once when it is defined. It does not have a constructor as it does not have a name. It cannot be static. The class definition ends with a semicolon.

d) **Static nested class** – these are inner classes marked as static inside an outer class. It cannot access non-static members of the outer class. You can access a static nested class without instantiating an object of outer class.

208: What is the difference between == and equals() in string comparison?

Answer:

If you need to compare the physical address of 2 string objects, the "==" operator can be used. If you only want to compare the values of 2 string objects, the equals() method is the best option.

For example:

String stringObj1 = "Hello";

String stringObj2 = "Hello";

System.out.println(stringObj1 == stringObj2); // this will print true as both stringObj1 and stringObj2 are pointing to the same object in the constant pool

String stringObj3 = new String("Hello");

System.out.println(stringObj1 == stringObj3); // this will print false as stringObj3 is a new instance of string

System.out.println(stringObj1.equals(stringObj3)); // this will print true since both the values are same

209: What is an Inner class?

Answer:

Inner class is a specialized class which allows you to declare one class within another class. In order to write a flexible, reusable, and maintainable code, you have to make the class as specialized. Just like the ordinary class, inner class also has methods and variables to assign and process data.

210: What are the types of classes available in Java?

Answer:

There are four types of classes available in Java. They are:

a) **Inner class:** This class is a non-static inner class declared within another class

b) **Static nested class:** This is a static inner class declared within another class

c) **Method-local inner class:** This class is declared within another class's method

d) **Anonymous inner class:** This class is declared within the method but without a name.

211: Write a compilable code that creates an instance of inner class from the outer class.

Answer:

The below code will create an instance of inner class from the outer class.

```java
class TestOuter {
        private int iValue = 100;
        public void callInner() {
                boolean isMyFile = false ;
                TestInner inner = new TestInner();
                Inner.readValue();
        }
        class TestInner {
                public void readValue() {
                        System.out.println("Value is : "+iValue);
                }
        }
}
```

In the above code, we have an inner class 'TestInner' which is instantiated from the outer class's (TestOuter) callInner() method.

212: Write two lines of code which will instantiate the inner class from the outer class.

Answer:

The below two lines of code will instantiate the inner class from the outer class.

> TestOuter outer = new TestOuter();
>
> TestOuter.TestInner inner = outer.new TestInner();

Since inner class is a non-static class, we can create an instance of inner class 'inner' by creating a reference (TestOuter.TestInner) of outer class.

213: Explain about "method-local" inner class.

Answer:

a) The "method-local" inner class is a type of inner class which is always defined inside the method of enclosing class.

b) This inner class has to be instantiated within the method but after class definition i.e., once we declare a class within the method, the class has to be instantiated inside the method itself but not outside the method.

c) This inner class uses only final variables within the method.

d) The only modifier that can be used with the "method-local" inner class is abstract and final.

214: What happens when you compile and execute the following line of code?

Runnable runnable = new Runnable();

Answer:

The above line of code will not compile because we are trying to instantiate an interface. It is not at all possible to instantiate an interface in Java.

215: Explain about anonymous inner class.

Answer:

The anonymous inner class can be better explained with the below example:

Runnable runnable = new Runnable() { //Line 1

    public void run() { } //Line 2

  }; //Line 3

  a) Anonymous inner class can either extend subclass or implement one interface but not both. In the above code, we have used Runnable interface as an anonymous inner class.

  b) This inner class has closed curly brace followed by semicolon as coded in Line 3. This is the syntax of declaring anonymous inner class.

  c) This inner class can have method which is from its reference sub class or interface. In the above code, we have used the run() method which belongs to the Runnable interface.

216: Write two lines of code and explain how will you

implement an anonymous inner class.

Answer:

The anonymous inner class has to be implemented by the following approach:

```
Runnable runnable = new Runnable() {
        public void run() { }
};
```

To implement an anonymous inner class, we can either use the Java interface or define our own interface or create subclasses and implement its methods.

In the above code, we have implemented the Java interface 'Runnable' and implemented its run() method. This is how we implement anonymous inner class in Java.

217: Explain about Static Nested classes.

Answer:

Static Nested class can be better explained with the below example:

```
class MyClass {
        int ivalue = 1000; //Line 1
        static class Nested { //Line 2
        }
}
```

The static class 'Nested' can be accessed as mentioned below:

```
MyClass.Nested nested = new MyClass.Nested();
```

a) As the name implies, the static inner class uses the static modifier as mentioned in line 2.

b) This is often not called as an inner class but this is a top level nested class. Since it is a top level nested class, it does not share the sources of outer class.

c) The static nested class also cannot access the non-static outer class variables i.e, the static class 'Nested' cannot access the 'MyClass' variable mentioned in Line 1.

218: Write a line of code and explain how will you instantiate the static nested class.

Answer:

The static nested class is instantiated as mentioned below:

MyClass.Nested nested = new MyClass.Nested();

To instantiate a "static nested" class, we need both the class name and the nested class name. In the above code, the class name is 'MyClass' and the "Static Nested" class name is 'Nested'. With the help of dot operator, the "static nested" class is instantiated.

219: Write a program and explain how will you declare method-local inner class.

Answer:

The "method-local" inner class has to be declared as below:

```
class TestOuter {
    private String strValue = "My String";
    public void callInner() {
        class TestInner { //Line 1
            public void readValue() {
                System.out.println("Value is : "+iValue);
            }
        }
```

```
TestInner inner = new TestInner(); //Line 2
inner.readValue();
}
}
```

The method-local inner class has to be declared within a method as mentioned in Line 1 in the above code. The method-local inner class 'TestInner' is instantiated within the method as mentioned in Line 2.

220: What are the valid modifiers of an inner class?

Answer:

Following are the valid modifiers of an inner class:

a) **public**: To provide access across applications

b) **private**: To provide access for a specific class

c) **protected**: To provide access for a specific package

d) **abstract**: To implement the feature of one object in another object

e) **final**: To declare object which should not be implemented in another object

f) **static**: (for static nested class) – To create one instance of the object

g) **strictfp**: To perform floating point math calculation

221: What are the various ways of assigning a string literal to a String variable?

Answer:

Following are the various ways of assigning a string literal to a string variable:

a)   String strValue1 = "String Literal 1";

b)   String strValue2 = new String("String Literal 2");

c)   String strValue3 = new String();
     strValue3 = "String Literal 3";

d)   String strValue4 = strValue3;

222: Which method is used to append a string literal to a String variable?

Answer:

String class has a method called concat() method which is used to append a string literal to a string variable.

The below lines of code explain how to append a string literal to a string variable:

> String strValue1 = "String Literal";
>
> strValue1 = strValue1.concat("Another Literal");

223: What will be the output when you compile and execute the following code?

String strValue = "Core";

strValue.concat(" Java"); //Line 1

System.out.println("The value of String is: "+strValue);

Answer:

On compiling and executing the above code, the output will be displayed as:

> The value of String is: Core

The reason is:

When we use concat() method, the value is appended to the string value. But in Line 1, the appended string is not assigned to the string reference 'strValue'. So, the value is displayed as above.

224: What are the most widely used methods of String class?

Answer:

The following are the most widely used methods of String class:

a) **concat():** This is used to append a string value

b) **length():** This is used to find the total characters available in a string

c) **replace():** This is used to replace a particular character or characters

d) **substring():** This is used to retrieve the particular character that exists in a position (Example: to retrieve 3rd character in a string)

e) **toString():** This is used to convert an integer or other type to a String

f) **trim():** This is used to remove the whitespaces in a string

g) **toUpperCase():** This is used to convert all the words of a string to upper case

h) **toLowerCase():** This is used to convert all the words of a string to lower case

i) **equalsIgnoreCase():** This is used to compare a string irrespective of a word that exists in upper case or lower case

j) **charAt():** This is used to retrieve a particular character in a string

225: When will you use String class and when will you use StringBuffer?

Answer:

When we have to handle lots of changes to the String object, we have to use StringBuffer. This is because if we use String class for string modification, lot of abandoned String objects will be left in the String pool which takes up lots of memory.

String class is used when it requires less or no modification because as explained above, using lots of string leads to add unwanted objects in memory.

226: How will you add string to a StringBuffer? Give an example.

Answer:

We can add string to a StringBuffer by the following approach:

```
StringBuffer stringBuffer = new StringBuffer();
stringBuffer.append("Core");
stringBuffer.append("Java");
```

String value is added to the StringBuffer using append() method and using new object as shown above.

227: What will be the output when you compile and execute the following code?

StringBuffer stringBuffer = new StringBuffer();

stringBuffer.append("Core");

stringBuffer.append("Java");

System.out.println("The resultant StringBuffer Value is: "+stringBuffer);

Answer:

On compiling and executing the above code, the output will be displayed as:

The resultant StringBuffer Value is: Core Java

In case of StringBuffer, the append method will concatenate the value with the previous value.

228: What is the difference between StringBuffer and StringBuilder?

Answer:

StringBuilder class has all the methods of StringBuffer but there is one difference between the two.

The StringBuilder is not thread safe i.e., StringBuilder methods are not synchronized. That means, StringBuilder should not be used when you execute two more threads in an application. Since StringBuilder methods are not synchronized, it can execute faster than StringBuffer.

229: Which class is preferred : StringBuffer or StringBuilder? Why?

Answer:

Since StringBuilder methods are not synchronized, StringBuilder can execute faster than StringBuffer. So, StringBuilder is more preferable than StringBuffer when you are not building thread-safe applications.

230: How will you assign a string literal in a StringBuilder and print its value from right to left?

Answer:

We can assign a string literal in StringBuilder by the below line of code:

StringBuilder sBuilder = new StringBuilder("Core Java");

The value of a string literal can be printed from right to left using reverse() method as shown below:

```
sBuilder.reverse();
System.out.println(sBuilder);
```

231: Is it possible to invoke chained methods in Java? If so, how will you invoke?

Answer:

Yes it is possible to invoke chain of methods in Java as shown below:

```
int iValue = callMethod1().callMethod2().callMethod3();
```

In the above code, the return type is int and it should be the same for all the methods.

232: What will be the value of the string object "yValue" from the below code?

String xValue = "xyz";

String yValue = xValue.concat("qrs").toUpperCase.replace('Z', 'c'); //Line 1

Answer:

On compiling and executing the above code, the value of "yValue" will be

XYcQRS

The above is an example of chained methods.

In the above code, in Line 1, the expression is executed from left to right.

First, xValue is concatenated to qrs and so the value becomes xyzqrs.

Then, the value is converted to Uppercase and so, the value becomes XYZQRS.

Then, the character Z is replaced with c and so, the value becomes ZYcQRS.

233: Have a look at the below code and explain how many reference variables and how many string objects will be available in the memory?

String sValue1 = "First Literal"; //Line 1

String sValue2 = sValue1;

sValue1 = sValue1.concat("Extra Stuff"); //Line 2

Answer:

The above code creates two reference variables and two string objects in memory.

The two reference variables are:

a) sValue1

b) sValue2

These are the declared String variables which are called as the reference variables.

The two string objects are:

a)   First Literal

b)   First LiteralExtra Stuff

Although from Line 1 it seems like we have assigned one value to sValue1 (1 object), in Line 3, we have used concat() method to append another value which actually creates another string object. So, there will be 2 string objects in memory.

This page is intentionally left blank.

Chapter 9

Streams

234: What are the different methods to create a java stream?

Answer:

Java streams can be created many ways. The following 5 methods are the easiest ways to create a stream:

    a)   Using Stream.of(val1, val2, val3....)

```
public class createStream {
    public static void main(String[] abc){
        Stream<Integer> stream = Stream.of(9,8,7,6,5,4,3,2,1);
        stream.forEach(cnt -> System.out.println(cnt));
    }
}
```

    b)   Using Stream.of(arrayOfValues)

```
public class createStream {
    public static void main(String[] abc){
```

```java
        Stream<Integer> stream = Stream.of( new
        integer[]{9,8,7,6,5,4,3,2,1} );
        stream.forEach(cnt -> System.out.println(cnt));
    }
}
```

c) Using aList.stream()

```java
public class createStream {
    public static void main(String[] abc){
        List<Integer> lst = new ArrayList<Integer>();
        for(int cnt = 1; cnt< 10; cnt++){
            lst.add(cnt);
        }
        Stream<Integer> stream1 = lst.stream();
        stream1.forEach(cnt1 -> System.out.println(cnt1));
    }
}
```

d) Using Stream.iterate()or Stream.generate() functions

```java
public class createStream {
    public static void main(String[] abc){
        Stream<Date> stream1 = Stream.generate(() -> { return
        new Date();});
        stream1.forEach(cnt -> System.out.println(cnt));
    }
}
```

e) Using String tokens or String chars

```java
public class createStream {
    public static void main(String[] abc){
        IntStream stream1 = "54321_gfedcba".chars();
        stream1.forEach(cnt -> System.out.println(cnt));
```

```
//OR
    Stream<String> stream1 =
    Stream.of("X$Y$Z".split("$"));
    stream1.forEach(cnt -> System.out.println(cnt));
}
}
```

235: What is the difference between streams and collections?

Answer:

Though Streams and Collections look similar, their functionality is very different. The major differences between Streams and Collections are:

a) Collection holds an array of values whereas streams do not hold any value. They only help us carry the source value through a pipeline of computations.

b) As they do not hold any value, they perform the function and do not change the value at source.

c) Collections are finite whereas strings are infinite

d) Streams performs mapping and other computations lazily which is more efficient

236: What is ParallelStream ?

Answer:

Java provides two key functionalities without having to configure specifically -

a) The JVM splits the data stream into several smaller streams so that it can be easily processed

b) Several streams of data are processed parallel

237: What is a forEach() method used for?

Answer:

The forEach () method is an iterator. Instead of explicitly writing a for-loop, the forEach () will perform the iteration.

238: What is the use of I/O streams?

Answer:

The I/O stream provides many classes and methods to read and write bytes, characters, arrays, and objects into a file and store it in the local or server file system. I/O stream is available from the beginning of the Java language introduction and is considered as the core API (Application Programming Interface) used to develop intranet and internet applications.

239: What happens when you execute the below line of code?
File myFile = new File("CoreJava.txt");

Answer:

When the above line of code is executed, the JVM creates an object called 'myFile' in the memory but the file CoreJava.txt will not be created. The file is actually created, only when you invoke the createNewFile() method.

240: Write a code that will create a file in the path
/usr/CoreJava.txt.

Answer:

Below code will create a file CoreJava.txt within the /usr/ directory:

```
import java.io.*;
```

```
class CreateFile {
    public static void main(String argument[]) {
        try {
            boolean isMyFile = false ;
            File txtFile = new File("/usr/CoreJava.txt"); // Line 1
            isMyFile = file.createNewFile(); //Line 2
        }
        catch (IOException exp) {
        }
    }
}
```

In the above code, when Line 1 is executed, an object 'txtFile' is created in memory and when Line 2 is executed, the file 'CoreJava.txt' is created inside the folder /usr/.

241: What is the use of File class?

Answer:

A File class is a higher level class which has methods to perform the following functions:

   a) Make new empty files

   b) Search files

   c) Delete files

   d) Create directories

   e) Get absolute path

242: What are the important methods of File class that are often used?

Answer:

We use the following methods of File class quite often:

    a) exists()

    b) createNewFile()

The return type of the first method is boolean. It returns true if the file exists and returns false if the file does not exist.

The return type of the second method is also boolean. If the file does not exist, this method with create a new file and if the file exists it will not create the file.

243: What is the use of FileReader class?

Answer:

FileReader class is used to read the contents of a file either by a single character, by a stream of whole characters or by fixed characters with the help of read() method.

They are usually wrapped within BufferedReader which provides performance improvement and more ways to process data.

For example:

```
try {
        File txtFile = new File("/usr/CoreJava.txt");
FileReader myFileReader = new FileReader(txtFile);
        totalCharInFile = myFileReader.read(totalChar); //Line 1
}catch (IOException exp) { }
```

In the above code, when Line 1 is executed, the read() method reads the content from the file CoreJava.txt.

244: What is the use of FileWriter class?

Answer:

FileWriter class is used to write characters or Strings in a file with the help of write() method.

They are usually wrapped within PrintWriter or BufferedWriter which provides performance improvement and more methods for writing data.

For example:

```
try {
        File txtFile = new File("/usr/CoreJava.txt");
        FileWriter myFileWriter = new FileWriter(txtFile);
        myFileWriter.write("Line 1 \n Line 2 \n); //Line 1
        myFileWriter.flush();
        myFileWriter.close();
}catch (IOException exp) { }
```

In the above code, when Line 1 is executed, the write() method writes the content into the file CoreJava.txt.

245: Write a code snippet that writes content in the file /usr/CoreJava.txt, reads the content from that file and displays the output in the console using FileWriter and FileReader.

Answer:

Below code snippet write contents in the file /usr/CoreJava.txt, reads contents from that file and displays the output in the console using FileWriter and FileReader class:

```
import java.io.*;
class CreateFile {
    public static void main(String argument[]) {
        char [] toatlChar = new char[1000];
        int totalCharInFile = 0;
```

```
try {
    File txtFile = new File("/usr/CoreJava.txt");
    FileWriter myFileWriter = new FileWriter(txtFile);
    myFileWriter.write("Line 1 \n Line 2 \n); //Line 1
    myFileWriter.flush();
    myFileWriter.close();

    FileReader myFileReader = new FileReader(txtFile);
    totalCharInFile = myFileReader.read(totalChar); //Line 2

    for(char readChar : totalChar) {
        System.out.print(readChar); //Line 3
    }

    myFileReader.close();

    }
    catch (IOException exp) {
    }
}
}
```

In the above code, when Line 1 is executed, the contents are written in the file CoreJava.txt.

When Line 2 is executed, the read() method reads the content from the file and gets the total number of characters.

The characters are then displayed when Line 3 is executed.

246: Write two lines of code that create a directory in the local

file system.

Answer:

The below two lines of code will create a directory in the local file system.

```
File myDirectory = new File("/usr/JavaCodes");
myDirectory.mkdir();
```

The first line creates an object and the second line creates an actual directory.

247: What happens when you compile and execute the code below? What will be the output?

```
File myDirectory = new File("/usr/JavaCodes");
File myNewFile = new File("/usr/JavaCodes/CoreJava.txt");
myNewFile.createNewFile();
```

Answer:

The above mentioned code will throw IOException because the directory /usr/JavaCodes/ is not created but only its object is created.

248: What is the use of BufferedReader class?

Answer:

Following are the uses of BufferedReader class:

a) It is used to read large amount of data

b) It keeps the data in a buffer so that the execution time is reduced and memory is saved

c) It has readLine() method to read the contents line by line from a file.

249: What is the use of BufferedWriter class?

Answer:

Following are the uses of BufferedWriter class:

a)   It is used to write large chunks of data at a single time

b)   It is used to automatically create OS specific line separators using newline() method.

250: Write four lines of code that will write contents in a file using PrintWriter class.

Answer:

The below four lines of code will write contents in a file using PrintWriter class.

```
File myNewFile = new File("/usr/CoreJava.txt");

PrintWriter myPrintWriter = new PrintWriter(myNewFile);
//Line 1

myPrintWriter.write("This gets inserted into the File"); //Line 2
myPrintWriter.flush();myPrintWriter.close(); //Line 3
```

In the above code, when Line 1 is executed, the file CoreJava.txt is created inside the folder /usr/.

When Line 2 is executed, the write() method writes the content in the file CoreJava.txt. When Line 3 is executed, the file is closed and the contents are stored in the file.

251: Write three lines of code to create and delete a file.

Answer:

The below three lines of code will create a file and delete a file from the file system.

```
File myNewFile = new File("/usr/CoreJava.txt");

myNewFile.createNewFile(); //Line 1
```

myNewFile.delete(); //Line 2

In the above code, when Line 1 is executed, the createNewFile() method creates the file CoreJava.txt inside the folder /usr/. When Line 2 is executed, the delete() method deletes the created file from the folder /usr/.

252: Which method is used to change the file name and directory? Give an example.

Answer:

renameTo() method is used to rename a file or a directory.

The below lines of code will rename a file from 'CoreJava.txt' to 'Java.txt'.

```
File myNewFile = new File("/usr/CoreJava.txt");
myNewFile.createNewFile();
File myAnotherFile = new File("/usr/Java.txt");
myNewFile.renameTo(myAnotherFile); //Line 1
```

The method renameTo() in Line 1 is used to rename a file from CoreJava.txt to Java.txt.

The below lines of code will rename a directory from 'JavaCodes' to 'MyJavaCodes'.

```
File myNewDirectory = new File("/usr/JavaCodes");
myNewDirectory.mkdir();
File myAnotherDirectory = new File("/usr/MyJavaCodes");
myNewDirectory.renameTo(myAnotherDirectory);
```

For renaming a directory, the same method renameTo() is used.

253: How will you define Serialization?

Answer:

Serialization is the process of storing object's state persistently to a byte stream. These bytes are used to convert them to live objects in future.

For example:

```
class Electronics implements Serializable {
        private int price; //Line 1
        public Electronics() {
                price = 10; //Line 2
        }
}
```

In the above code, the value of price in Line 2 is stored as stream of bytes i.e., the value of price will be stored as 1010.

254: Which methods are used to serialize and de-serialize objects?

Answer:

The writeObject() method of ObjectOutputStream class is used to serialize objects.

The readObject() method of ObjectInputStream class is used to de-serialize objects.

255: What is the use of transient keyword?

Answer:

The transient keyword is used to declare an instance variable. If we make the variable as transient, then the variable will never be serialized although the methods in the objects are serializable.

For example:

```
class Electronics implements Serializable {
```

```
transient private int price; //Line 1
public Electronics(int totalPrice) {
        price = totalPrice;
        int priceElectronics = totalPrice;
    }
}
```

In the above code, Line 1 is not serialized although the object 'priceElectronics' which exists inside the method Electronics() is serializable.

256: How will you use serialization in your code?

Answer:

We have to implement the serializable interface for object serialization (which is nothing but converting data into stream of bytes).

For example:

```
class Electronics implements Serializable {
        private int price;
        public Electronics(int totalPrice) {
                price = totalPrice;
            }
}
```

257: What are the methods of Serializable interface?

Answer:

The Serializable interface has no methods for implementation. If a super class is serializable then its sub class is also serializable.

258: What is the use of ObjectOutputStream?

Answer:

ObjectOutputStream is a higher level class in the Java IO package which is mainly used to wrap the lower level Class FileOutputStream, serialize the objects and write them into a stream.

It supports the below method:

ObjectOutputStream.writeObject()

The above method will serialize the object and write the contents into a Stream.

259: What is the use of ObjectInputStream?

Answer:

ObjectInputStream is a higher level class in the Java IO package which is mainly used to wrap the lower level Class FileInputStream, read the stream and de-serialize the objects.

It supports the below method:

ObjectInputStream.readObject();

The above readObject() method reads the stream of contents and de-serializes the object.

260: What will be the output when you compile the code below?

```
import java.io.*;
public class TestSeriazation {
    public static void main(String argument[]) {
        MySerial mySerial = new MySerial();
        try {
        ObjectOutputStream oStream = new ObjectOutputStream (new
```

```
        FileOutputStream("myNewFile");
oStream.writeObject(mySerial); oStream.close();
system.out.print(++mySerial.sValue + " "); //L1


ObjectInputStream iStream = new ObjectInputStream (new
        FileInputStream("myNewFile");
MySerial mySerial2 = (MySerial) iStream.readObject();
iStream.close();
System.out.println(mySerial2.tValue + " " +
mySerial2.sValue);//L2
}
catch(Exception exp) {
        System.out.println("Exception: " );
}
}
}
class MySerial implements Serializable {
    transient tValue = 100;
    static int sValue = 100;
    }
```

Answer:

The code compiles fine and it prints the following output:

        101 0 101

In the above code, when line L1 is executed, the value of sValue becomes 101 and it is printed as displayed above. When Line L2 is executed, the value of tValue is 0 and sValue is 101 which are printed as above. So, it is clear that, we can override readObject() method in order to change the default de-serialization process.

261: Which of the following lines will compile and which will not?

BufferedWriter bw1=new BufferedWriter(new FileWriter("myNewFile1")); //L 1

BufferedWriter bw2=new BufferedWriter(new BufferedWriter(bw)); //L 2

BufferedWriter bw3=new BufferedWriter(new File("myNewFile3")); //L 3

BufferedWriter bw4=new BufferedWriter(new PrintWriter("myNewFile4")); //L4

Answer:

In Line 2, bw is a reference to BufferedWriter.

The lines L 1, L 3, and L 4 will compile and the line L 2 will not compile. This is because, BufferedWriter which is also called as a decorator class is mainly used to extend the functionality of the other classes but it is not used to write object. So, L2 will not compile. All the other lines L1, L3, and L4 compile fine and will create a new file.

262: What will be the output of the following code?

```java
import java.io.*;
public class Electronics implements Serializable{
    public static void main(String argument[]) {
        private Camera camera = new Camera();
        Electronics electronics = new Electronics ();
        electronics.storeData(camera);
    }
    public void storeData(Electronics electronics) {
        try {
```

```
ObjectOutputStream oStream = new ObjectOutputStream (new
    FileOutputStream("myNewFile");
oStream.writeObject(electronics); oStream.close();
System.out.println("Camera added to file.");
}
catch(Exception exp) {
    System.out.println("Exception: ");
}
}
}
```

Answer:

The above code prints the below output:

Exception:

The code throws an exception. This is because the class Camera does not implement the serializable interface. All the instances of a serializable object must also be serialized. If an instance of a serializable object is not serialized, it will throw an exception.

This page is intentionally left blank.

Chapter 10

Collections

263: What are the four interfaces of Java collections?

Answer:

Collection is that the root of the collection hierarchy. A collection incorporates a multitude of objects cited as its elements. The Java platform doesn't give any direct implementations of this interface.

Set can be a collection that contains distinctive elements. This interface is used to represent data similar to the deck of cards.

List is a collection which is ordered and it will allow duplicate elements also. You may be able to access any part from its index. List is more like array with variable length.

A **Map** matches keys to values. A map will not contain duplicate keys: every key can map to at the most one value.

264: List the differences between the Iterator and Enumeration interfaces?

Answer:

Enumeration is double as quick as Iterator and uses very less memory.

Enumeration is extremely basic and fits to basic wants. However Iterator is far safer as compared to Enumeration because it continuously denies different threads to change the collection object that is being iterated by it.

Iterator takes the place of Enumeration within the Java Collections Framework. Iterators permit the caller to get rid of parts from the underlying collection that's unacceptable with Enumeration.

265: What are the common algorithms implemented in Collections Framework?

Answer:

Java Collections Framework provides algorithmic rule implementations that are ordinarily used like sorting and searching. Collections class contain these functional implementations. Most of those algorithms work on List however a number of them are applicable for every kind of collections. Some of them are sort, search, shuffle, min and max values etc.

266: Assume that you have added all the employee names that are available in Database to a list. How will you display the employee names in natural order?

Answer:

Natural order refers to alphabetical order. Based on the

assumption that list has all the employee names, the code has to be written as

ArrayList employeeList = new ArrayList();

employeeList.add(employeeName);

Now, employeeList holds all the employee names.

To display the employee names in ascending order, we have to invoke collection's sort method as shown below.

Collections.sort(employeeList);

System.out.println("Sorted List: "+employeeList);

267: Explain about Queue interface.

Answer:

Queue interface is used to hold a list of to-Dos.

Queue is typically considered as FIFO (First in First Out).

Queue supports all of the standard Collection methods to add and review queue elements.

268: Which collection would you choose, if you need to keep track of which employee was last accessed from the collection? Explain about its iteration speed.

Answer:

We will choose LinkedHashMap because LinkedHashMap maintains the insertion order or access order of an object.

The iteration of LinkedHashMap is faster but the addition and removal of elements are slower when compared to HashMap.

269: Which feature of Java is used to convert primitive type to reference type?

Answer:

Java uses Autoboxing feature to convert a primitive type to a reference type. The below 2 lines of code is an example for manual way of converting primitive to a reference type.

> List intList = new ArrayList();
>
> intList.add(new Integer(10)); //Line 2

The below line is an example for Autoboxing:

> intList.add(10);

270: What are the points you need to remember when you override equals() and compareTo() method?

Answer:

When you override the equals() method, you must pass an argument of type Object as shown below which otherwise will throw a compilation error.

> public boolean equals(Object myObject);

When you override the compareTo() method, you must pass an argument of the type you are sorting.

For example:

> Float fValue1 = 10.0f;
>
> Float fValue2 = 10.0F;
>
> System.out.println(fValue1.compareTo(fValue2));

The above displays the output as 0. This is because, compareTo method returns 0 if both the values are equal.

271: How will you search for a specific element in collection?

Answer:

We have to use Arrays.binarySearch() method to search for a

specific element in an array or collection. This method returns the index of the particular searched element.

For example:

    String [] strArr = {"one", "two", "four"};

    Arrays.sort(strArr);

    System.out.println("Sorted Order: "+ strArr);

    System.out.println("Search index of one is:

    "+Arrays.binarySearch(strArr, "one"));

The output will be returned as :

Sorted Order: four

    one

    two

Search index of one is: 1

272: How will you define a reflexive equals() contract?

Answer:

The equals() contract is said to be reflexive if the objects are equal and returns true in all the cases:

For example, consider the below lines of code:

    Object v1; Object v2;

    v1.equals(v2);

i.e., for any reference variable v1, v1.equals(v2) always returns true for reflexive contract.

273: Which collection would you choose if you want no duplicates and if objects are not stored in an order?

Answer:

We have to choose HashSet as we dont not want duplicate objects getting stored in a collection. It is an unsorted and unordered set. The performance of HashSet is better than LinkedHashSet and TreeSet because HashSet uses hashCode() method which is mainly used to identify the hash value of the object being inserted.

274: How will you use the Comparator interface in your class file?

Answer:

We have to use Comparator interface in a class by using the 'implements' keyword. We also need to override its compare() method.

Below is the example code snippet:

```
class PerformSort implements Comparator<String> {
        public int compare(String strOne, String strTwo) {
                return strTwo.compareTo(strOne);
        }
}
```

275: Explain symmetric equals() contract.

Answer:

Assume that there are two objects v1 and v2. v1 is equal to v2, if and only if v2 is equal to v1. This equals() contract is called as symmetric contract.

For example, consider the below lines of code:

```
Object v1; Object v2;
v1.equals(v2); //Line 1
v2.equals(v1); //Line 2
```

So, in case of symmetric contract, Line 1 returns true if and only if

Line 2 returns true.

276: How will you review the queue of a collection object?

Answer:

We have to use any of the below methods of PriorityQueue class to review the queue of an object.

a) **offer(E e):** This adds an object to the queue. It does not throw an Exception if it is not possible to add the object to the queue.

b) **peek():** This returns the last added object in the queue

c) **pool():** This returns the first added object in the queue

d) **remove(Object O):** This removes the object from the queue

e) **add(E e):** This adds an object to the queue. This method throws an Exception if it is not possible to add the object to the queue.

277: Is it possible to mix generic and non-generic collections? If so, give example.

Answer:

Yes, it is possible to mix generic and non-generic collections. The example for this is shown below.

```
public class TestGenericAndNonGeneric {
        public static void main(String argument[]) {
                List<Float> addList = new ArrayList<Float>();
                addList.add(2.0); // Line 1
                addList.add(4.0); //Line 2
                InsertNewRecord ir = new InsertNewRecord();
```

```
                ir.insertValue(myList);
        }
}
public class InsertNewRecord {
        void insertValue(List addMyList) { //Line 3
                addMyList.add(new String("3"); //Line 4
        }
}
```

In the above code, in Line 1 and Line 2, we have added float literal to the list which is a generic float collection.

In Line 4, we have added a string literal to the list object which is a non-generic collection because the type is not defined while declaring the object 'addMyList' in Line 3.

278: Explain transitive equals() contract.

Answer:

The equals() contract is said to be transitive for the below scenario:
For any reference variable v1, v2, and v3, if v1.equals(v2) returns true and if v2.equals(v3) returns true, then v1.equals(v3) must return true.

For example:

```
        Object v1; Object v2; Object v3;
        boolean bValue1 = v1.equals(v2); //Line 1
        boolean bValue2 = v2.equals(v3); //Line 2
        boolean bValue3 = v1.equals(v3); //Line 3
```

In the above code, Line 3 returns true, if and only if Line 1 and Line 2 return true. This is called as transitive equals contract.

279: What happens when you compile and run the following code?

class Mammal {}

class Cat extends Mammal { }

List<Mammal> list = new ArrayList<Cat>();

Answer:

The code will not compile. The rule is that the type of the variable declaration must match the type that you pass to the actual data type.

280: Will the following line of code compile without error? If not, state the reasons.

List<?> list = new ArrayList<? extends Mammal>();

Answer:

The above line of code will not compile because in the above line, to declare the object 'list', we have used the wild card notation '?'. The wild card notation '?' cannot be used for object creation.

281: Assume that we have a String array containing five elements. What will be the range of results if we make a search on the string array? State the reasons for the same.

Answer:

The range of results will be from -6 through 4. This is because, the search will return the index of the element if it is matched. If the element is not matched, the search will return a negative number that if it is inverted and decremented, gives you the insertion point (the index) at which the value searched on should be inserted into the array.

282: Will the following line of code compile without error? If not, state the reasons.

List<? super Mammal> mList = new ArrayList<Cat>();

Answer:

The above line of code will not compile because the class hierarchy of Cat is very low. Since Mammal is declared as a super class, if <Cat> is replaced with <Mammal> or <Object>, then the above line will be considered as legal.

283: Assume that we have a below method

public void getList(T t)

In order for the method to be legal, what should exist?

Answer:

The only way for the above method is to be legal is, there should exist a class named T where the argument must be declared like any other type declaration for a variable. This is an example for creating generic method.

284: What are the activities that can be performed in collection API?

Answer:

In collection API we could perform the following activities.

    a)   Add objects

    b)   Remove objects

    c)   Verify object inclusion

    d)   Retrieve objects and

    e)   Iterate

285: In collection, which method is used to remove the head of the queue?

Answer:

The interface Queue has a method called poll() which is used to remove the head of the queue irrespective of the element order.

For example:

```
Int iValue = 1000;
String strValue = "Java";
LinkedList lList = new LinkedList();
lList.add(iValue); lList.add(strValue);
System.out.println("The Element removed is:
"+lList.poll()) // Line 1
```

In the above code, when Line 1 is executed, it displays the output as

The Element removed is: 1000

The reason is, poll() method always removes the head of the queue i.e., the first element added in the queue.

286: Which collection class method is not synchronized but allows growing or shrinking its size and provides indexed access to its elements?

Answer:

ArrayList (which is used to store objects in an array) class that belongs to java.util package is the only collection class that allows growing or shrinking its size, provides indexed access to its elements and its methods are not synchronized.

287: How will you define a consistent equals() contract?

Answer:

The equals() contract is said to be consistent if the object returns either true or false:

For example, consider the the below lines of code:

> Varibale v1; Variable v2;

> v1.equals(v2);

So, in case of consistent contract, multiple invocations of v1.equals(v2) consistently return true or it consistently returns false. But no information that is used in the equals() method gets modified.

288: How will you extract elements from a collection without knowing how the collection is implemented?
Answer:

In Java, java.util.Enumeration interface is used to extract elements one by one from a collection without the need to know how the collection is implemented.

The Enumeration interface has two methods

a) **boolean hasMoreElements():** This is used to check if elements exist

b) **Object nextElement():** This is used to extract the element value

289: In collection, which classes and interfaces support event handling?
Answer:

In collection, EventObject class and EventListener interface are used to support event handling which is also called as event processing.

EventObject is a root class of all the event objects (ChangeEvent, MenuEvent, PrintEvent, etc.) which belongs to java.util package.

EvenListener interface is the root of all the listener interfaces (ActionListener, EventListener, FocusListener, etc.) All the listener interfaces must extend the EventListener interface for event handling.

290: How will you access locale specific resources in Java?
Answer:

In Java, we have ResourceBundle class contains locale specific objects. So, in your program, if you need locale specific resources, you have to load it from the ResourceBundle class that is appropriate for the current user's locale.

The ResourceBundle contains key value pair in which the keys are used to uniquely identify a locale specific object in the bundle.

This page is intentionally left blank.

HR Questions

Review these typical interview questions and think about how you would answer them. Read the answers listed; you will find best possible answers along with strategies and suggestions.

1: Where do you find ideas?

Answer:

Ideas can come from all places, and an interviewer wants to see that your ideas are just as varied. Mention multiple places that you gain ideas from, or settings in which you find yourself brainstorming. Additionally, elaborate on how you record ideas or expand upon them later.

2: How do you achieve creativity in the workplace?

Answer:

It's important to show the interviewer that you're capable of being resourceful and innovative in the workplace, without stepping outside the lines of company values. Explain where ideas normally stem from for you (examples may include an exercise such as list-making or a mind map), and connect this to a particular task in your job that it would be helpful to be creative in.

3: How do you push others to create ideas?

Answer:

If you're in a supervisory position, this may be requiring employees to submit a particular number of ideas, or to complete regular idea-generating exercises, in order to work their creative muscles. However, you can also push others around you to create ideas simply by creating more of your own. Additionally, discuss with the interviewer the importance of questioning people as a way to inspire ideas and change.

4: Describe your creativity.

Answer:

Try to keep this answer within the professional realm, but if you have an impressive background in something creative outside of your employment history, don't be afraid to include it in your answer also. The best answers about creativity will relate problem-solving skills, goal-setting, and finding innovative ways to tackle a project or make a sale in the workplace. However, passions outside of the office are great, too (so long as they don't cut into your work time or mental space).

5: Would you rather receive more authority or more responsibility at work?

Answer:

There are pros and cons to each of these options, and your interviewer will be more interested to see that you can provide a critical answer to the question. Receiving more authority may mean greater decision-making power and may be great for those with outstanding leadership skills, while greater responsibility may be a growth opportunity for those looking to advance steadily throughout their careers.

6: What do you do when someone in a group isn't contributing their fair share?

Answer:

This is a particularly important question if you're interviewing for a position in a supervisory role – explain the ways in which you would identify the problem, and how you would go about pulling aside the individual to discuss their contributions. It's important to understand the process of creating a dialogue, so that you can communicate your expectations clearly to the individual, give them a chance to respond, and to make clear what needs to change. After this, create an action plan with the group member to ensure their contributions are on par with others in the group.

7: Tell me about a time when you made a decision that was outside of your authority.

Answer:

While an answer to this question may portray you as being decisive and confident, it could also identify you to an employer as a potential problem employee. Instead, it may be best to slightly refocus the question into an example of a time that you took on additional responsibilities, and thus had to make decisions that were outside of your normal authority (but which had been granted to you in the specific instance). Discuss how the weight of the decision affected your decision-making process, and the outcomes of the situation.

8: Are you comfortable going to supervisors with disputes?

Answer:

If a problem arises, employers want to know that you will handle it in a timely and appropriate manner. Emphasize that you've rarely had disputes with supervisors in the past, but if a situation were to arise, you feel perfectly comfortable in discussing it with the person in question in order to find a resolution that is satisfactory to both parties.

9: If you had been in charge at your last job, what would you have done differently?

Answer:

No matter how many ideas you have about how things could run better, or opinions on the management at your previous job, remain positive when answering this question. It's okay to show thoughtful reflection on how something could be handled in order to increase efficiency or improve sales, but be sure to keep all of your suggestions focused on making things better, rather than talking about ways to eliminate waste or negativity.

10: Do you believe employers should praise or reward employees for a job well done?

Answer:

Recognition is always great after completing a difficult job, but there are many employers who may ask this question as a way to infer as to whether or not you'll be a high-maintenance worker. While you may appreciate rewards or praise, it's important to convey to the interviewer that you don't require accolades to be confident that you've done your job well. If you are interviewing for a supervisory position where you would be the one praising other employees, highlight the importance of praise in boosting team morale.

11: What do you believe is the most important quality a leader can have?

Answer:

There are many important skills for a leader to have in any

business, and the most important component of this question is that you explain why the quality you choose to highlight is important. Try to choose a quality such as communication skills, or an ability to inspire people, and relate it to a specific instance in which you displayed the quality among a team of people.

12: Tell me about a time when an unforeseen problem arose. How did you handle it?

Answer:

It's important that you are resourceful, and level-headed under pressure. An interviewer wants to see that you handle problems systematically, and that you can deal with change in an orderly process. Outline the situation clearly, including all solutions and results of the process you implemented.

13: Can you give me an example of a time when you were able to improve X objective at your previous job?

Answer:

It's important here to focus on an improvement you made that created tangible results for your company. Increasing efficiency is certainly a very important element in business, but employers are also looking for concrete results such as increased sales or cut expenses. Explain your process thoroughly, offering specific numbers and evidence wherever possible, particularly in outlining the results.

14: Tell me about a time when a supervisor did not provide specific enough direction on a project.

Answer:

While many employers want their employees to follow very specific guidelines without much decision-making power, it's important also to be able to pick up a project with vague direction and to perform self-sufficiently. Give examples of necessary questions that you asked, and specify how you determined whether a question was something you needed to ask of a supervisor or whether it was something you could determine on your own.

15: Tell me about a time when you were in charge of leading a project.

Answer:

Lead the interviewer through the process of the project, just as you would have with any of your team members. Explain the goal of the project, the necessary steps, and how you delegated tasks to your team. Include the results, and what you learned as a result of the leadership opportunity.

16: Tell me about a suggestion you made to a former employer that was later implemented.

Answer:

Employers want to see that you're interested in improving your company and doing your part – offer a specific example of something you did to create a positive change in your previous job. Explain how you thought of the idea, how your supervisors received it, and what other employees thought was the idea was put into place.

17: Tell me about a time when you thought of a way something in the workplace could be done more efficiently.

Answer:

Focus on the positive aspects of your idea. It's important not to portray your old company or boss negatively, so don't elaborate on how inefficient a particular system was. Rather, explain a situation in which you saw an opportunity to increase productivity or to streamline a process, and explain in a general step-by-step how you implemented a better system.

18: Is there a difference between leading and managing people – which is your greater strength?

Answer:

There is a difference – leaders are often great idea people, passionate, charismatic, and with the ability to organize and inspire others, while managers are those who ensure a system runs, facilitate its operations, make authoritative decisions, and who take great responsibility for all aspects from overall success to the finest decisions. Consider which of these is most applicable to the position, and explain how you fit into this role, offering concrete examples of your past experience.

19: Do you function better in a leadership role, or as a worker on a team?

Answer:

It is important to consider what qualities the interviewer is looking for in your position, and to express how you embody this role. If you're a leader, highlight your great ideas, drive and passion, and ability to incite others around you to action. If you work great in teams, focus on your dedication to the task at hand, your cooperation and communication skills, and your ability to keep things running smoothly.

20: Tell me about a time when you discovered something in the workplace that was disrupting your (or others) productivity – what did you do about it?

Answer:

Try to not focus on negative aspects of your previous job too much, but instead choose an instance in which you found a positive, and quick, solution to increase productivity. Focus on the way you noticed the opportunity, how you presented a solution to your supervisor, and then how the change was implemented (most importantly, talk about how you led the change initiative). This is a great opportunity for you to display your problem-solving skills, as well as your resourceful nature and leadership skills.

21: How do you perform in a job with clearly-defined objectives and goals?

Answer:

It is important to consider the position when answering this question – clearly, it is best if you can excel in a job with clearly-defined objectives and goals (particularly if you're in an entry level or sales position). However, if you're applying for a position with a leadership role or creative aspect to it, be sure to focus on the ways that you additionally enjoy the challenges of developing and implementing your own ideas.

22: How do you perform in a job where you have great decision-making power?

Answer:

The interviewer wants to know that, if hired, you won't be the type of employee who needs constant supervision or who asks for advice, authority, or feedback every step of the way. Explain that you work well in a decisive, productive environment, and that you look forward to taking initiative in your position.

23: If you saw another employee doing something dishonest or unethical, what would you do?

Answer:

In the case of witnessing another employee doing something dishonest, it is always best to act in accordance with company policies for such a situation – and if you don't know what this company's specific policies are, feel free to simply state that you would handle it according to the policy and by reporting it to the appropriate persons in charge. If you are aware of the company's policies (such as if you are seeking a promotion within your own company), it is best to specifically outline your actions according to the policy.

24: Tell me about a time when you learned something on your own that later helped in your professional life.

Answer:

This question is important because it allows the interviewer to gain insight into your dedication to learning and advancement. Choose an example solely from your personal life, and provide a brief anecdote ending in the lesson you learned. Then, explain in a clear and thorough manner how this lesson has translated into a usable skill or practice in your position.

25: Tell me about a time when you developed a project idea at work.

Answer:

Choose a project idea that you developed that was typical of projects you might complete in the new position. Outline where your idea came from, the type of research you did to ensure its success and relevancy, steps that were included in the project, and the end results. Offer specific before and after statistics, to show its success.

26: Tell me about a time when you took a risk on a project.

Answer:

Whether the risk involved something as complex as taking on a major project with limited resources or time, or simply volunteering for a task that was outside your field of experience, show that you are willing to stretch out of your comfort zone and to try new things. Offer specific examples of why something you did was risky, and explain what you learned in the process – or how this prepared you for a job objective you later faced in your career.

27: What would you tell someone who was looking to get into

this field?

Answer:

This question allows you to be the expert – and will show the interviewer that you have the knowledge and experience to go along with any training and education on your resume. Offer your knowledge as advice of unexpected things that someone entering the field may encounter, and be sure to end with positive advice such as the passion or dedication to the work that is required to truly succeed.

28: Tell me about a time when you didn't meet a deadline.

Answer:

Ideally, this hasn't happened – but if it has, make sure you use a minor example to illustrate the situation, emphasize how long ago it happened, and be sure that you did as much as you could to ensure that the deadline was met. Additionally, be sure to include what you learned about managing time better or prioritizing tasks in order to meet all future deadlines.

29: How do you eliminate distractions while working?

Answer:

With the increase of technology and the ease of communication, new distractions arise every day. Your interviewer will want to see that you are still able to focus on work, and that your productivity has not been affected, by an example showing a routine you employ in order to stay on task.

30: Tell me about a time when you worked in a position with a

weekly or monthly quota to meet. **How often were you successful?**

Answer:

Your numbers will speak for themselves, and you must answer this question honestly. If you were regularly met your quotas, be sure to highlight this in a confident manner and don't be shy in pointing out your strengths in this area. If your statistics are less than stellar, try to point out trends in which they increased toward the end of your employment, and show reflection as to ways you can improve in the future.

31: Tell me about a time when you met a tough deadline, and how you were able to complete it.

Answer:

Explain how you were able to prioritize tasks, or to delegate portions of an assignments to other team members, in order to deal with a tough deadline. It may be beneficial to specify why the deadline was tough – make sure it's clear that it was not a result of procrastination on your part. Finally, explain how you were able to successfully meet the deadline, and what it took to get there in the end.

32: How do you stay organized when you have multiple projects on your plate?

Answer:

The interviewer will be looking to see that you can manage your time and work well – and being able to handle multiple projects at once, and still giving each the attention it deserves, is a great mark of a worker's competence and efficiency. Go through a typical process of goal-setting and prioritizing, and explain the steps of these to the interviewer, so he or she can see how well you manage time.

33: How much time during your work day do you spend on "auto-pilot?"

Answer:

While you may wonder if the employer is looking to see how efficient you are with this question (for example, so good at your job that you don't have to think about it), but in almost every case, the employer wants to see that you're constantly thinking, analyzing, and processing what's going on in the workplace. Even if things are running smoothly, there's usually an opportunity somewhere to make things more efficient or to increase sales or productivity. Stress your dedication to ongoing development, and convey that being on "auto-pilot" is not conducive to that type of success.

34: How do you handle deadlines?

Answer:

The most important part of handling tough deadlines is to prioritize tasks and set goals for completion, as well as to delegate or eliminate unnecessary work. Lead the interviewer through a general scenario, and display your competency through your ability to organize and set priorities, and most importantly, remain calm.

35: Tell me about your personal problem-solving process.

Answer:

Your personal problem-solving process should include outlining the problem, coming up with possible ways to fix the problem, and setting a clear action plan that leads to resolution. Keep your answer brief and organized, and explain the steps in a concise, calm manner that shows you are level-headed even under stress.

36: What sort of things at work can make you stressed?

Answer:

As it's best to stay away from negatives, keep this answer brief and simple. While answering that nothing at work makes you stressed will not be very believable to the interviewer, keep your answer to one generic principle such as when members of a team don't keep their commitments, and then focus on a solution you generally employ to tackle that stress, such as having weekly status meetings or intermittent deadlines along the course of a project.

37: What do you look like when you are stressed about something? How do you solve it?

Answer:

This is a trick question – your interviewer wants to hear that you don't look any different when you're stressed, and that you don't allow negative emotions to interfere with your productivity. As far as how you solve your stress, it's best if you have a simple solution mastered, such as simply taking deep breaths and counting to 10 to bring yourself back to the task at hand.

38: Can you multi-task?
Answer:

Some people can, and some people can't. The most important part of multi-tasking is to keep a clear head at all times about what needs to be done, and what priority each task falls under. Explain how you evaluate tasks to determine priority, and how you manage your time in order to ensure that all are completed efficiently.

39: How many hours per week do you work?
Answer:

Many people get tricked by this question, thinking that answering more hours is better – however, this may cause an employer to wonder why you have to work so many hours in order to get the work done that other people can do in a shorter amount of time. Give a fair estimate of hours that it should take you to complete a job, and explain that you are also willing to work extra whenever needed.

40: How many times per day do you check your email?
Answer:

While an employer wants to see that you are plugged into modern technology, it is also important that the number of times you check your email per day is relatively low – perhaps two to three times per day (dependent on the specific field you're in). Checking email is often a great distraction in the workplace, and while it is important to remain connected, much correspondence can simply be handled together in the morning and afternoon.

41: What is customer service?

Answer:

Customer service can be many things – and the most important consideration in this question is that you have a creative answer. Demonstrate your ability to think outside the box by offering a confident answer that goes past a basic definition, and that shows you have truly considered your own individual view of what it means to take care of your customers. The thoughtful consideration you hold for customers will speak for itself.

42: Tell me about a time when you went out of your way for a customer.

Answer:

It's important that you offer an example of a time you truly went out of your way – be careful not to confuse something that felt like a big effort on your part, with something your employer would expect you to do anyway. Offer an example of the customer's problems, what you did to solve it, and the way the customer responded after you took care of the situation.

43: How do you gain confidence from customers?

Answer:

This is a very open-ended question that allows you to show your customer service skills to the interviewer. There are many possible answers, and it is best to choose something that you've had great experience with, such as "by handling situations with transparency," "offering rewards," or "focusing on great communication." Offer specific examples of successes you've had.

44: Tell me about a time when a customer was upset or agitated – how did you handle the situation?

Answer:

Similarly to handling a dispute with another employee, the most important part to answering this question is to first set up the scenario, offer a step-by-step guide to your particular conflict resolution style, and end by describing the way the conflict was resolved. Be sure that in answering questions about your own conflict resolution style, that you emphasize the importance of open communication and understanding from both parties, as well as a willingness to reach a compromise or other solution.

45: When can you make an exception for a customer?

Answer:

Exceptions for customers can generally be made when in accordance with company policy or when directed by a supervisor. Display an understanding of the types of situations in which an exception should be considered, such as when a customer has endured a particular hardship, had a complication with an order, or at a request.

46: What would you do in a situation where you were needed by both a customer and your boss?

Answer:

While both your customer and your boss have different needs of you and are very important to your success as a worker, it is always best to try to attend to your customer first – however, the key is explaining to your boss why you are needed urgently by the customer, and then to assure your boss that you will attend to his or her needs as soon as possible (unless it's absolutely an urgent matter).

47: What is the most important aspect of customer service?

Answer:

While many people would simply state that customer satisfaction is the most important aspect of customer service, it's important to be able to elaborate on other important techniques in customer service situations. Explain why customer service is such a key part of business, and be sure to expand on the aspect that you deem to be the most important in a way that is reasoned and well-thought out.

48: Is it best to create low or high expectations for a customer?

Answer:

You may answer this question either way (after, of course, determining that the company does not have a clear opinion on the matter). However, no matter which way you answer the question, you must display a thorough thought process, and very clear reasoning for the option you chose. Offer pros and cons of each, and include the ultimate point that tips the scale in favor of your chosen answer.

49: Describe a time when you communicated a difficult or complicated idea to a coworker.

Answer:

Start by explaining the idea briefly to the interviewer, and then

give an overview of why it was necessary to break it down further
to the coworker. Finally, explain the idea in succinct steps, so the
interviewer can see your communication abilities and skill in
simplification.

50: What situations do you find it difficult to communicate in?
Answer:

Even great communicators will often find particular situations
that are more difficult to communicate effectively in, so don't be
afraid to answer this question honestly. Be sure to explain why
the particular situation you name is difficult for you, and try to
choose an uncommon answer such as language barrier or in time
of hardship, rather than a situation such as speaking to someone
of higher authority.

51: What are the key components of good communication?
Answer:

Some of the components of good communication include an
environment that is free from distractions, feedback from the
listener, and revision or clarification from the speaker when
necessary. Refer to basic communication models where necessary,
and offer to go through a role-play sample with the interviewer in
order to show your skills.

52: Tell me about a time when you solved a problem through communication?
Answer:

Solving problems through communication is key in the business world, so choose a specific situation from your previous job in which you navigated a messy situation by communicating effectively through the conflict. Explain the basis of the situation, as well as the communication steps you took, and end with a discussion of why communicating through the problem was so important to its resolution.

53: Tell me about a time when you had a dispute with another employee. How did you resolve the situation?

Answer:

Make sure to use a specific instance, and explain step-by-step the scenario, what you did to handle it, and how it was finally resolved. The middle step, how you handled the dispute, is clearly the most definitive – describe the types of communication you used, and how you used compromise to reach a decision. Conflict resolution is an important skill for any employee to have, and is one that interviewers will search for to determine both how likely you are to be involved in disputes, and how likely they are to be forced to become involved in the dispute if one arises.

54: Do you build relationships quickly with people, or take more time to get to know them?

Answer:

Either of these options can display good qualities, so determine which style is more applicable to you. Emphasize the steps you take in relationship-building over the particular style, and summarize briefly why this works best for you.

55: Describe a time when you had to work through office politics to solve a problem.

Answer:

Try to focus on the positives in this question, so that you can use the situation to your advantage. Don't portray your previous employer negatively, and instead use a minimal instance (such as paperwork or a single individual), to highlight how you worked through a specific instance resourcefully. Give examples of communication skills or problem-solving you used in order to achieve a resolution.

56: Tell me about a time when you persuaded others to take on a difficult task?

Answer:

This question is an opportunity to highlight both your leadership and communication skills. While the specific situation itself is important to offer as background, focus on how you were able to persuade the others, and what tactics worked the best.

57: Tell me about a time when you successfully persuaded a group to accept your proposal.

Answer:

This question is designed to determine your resourcefulness and your communication skills. Explain the ways in which you took into account different perspectives within the group, and created a presentation that would be appealing and convincing to all members. Additionally, you can pump up the proposal itself by offering details about it that show how well-executed it was.

58: Tell me about a time when you had a problem with another person, that, in hindsight, you wished you had handled differently.

Answer:

The key to this question is to show your capabilities of reflection and your learning process. Explain the situation, how you handled it at the time, what the outcome of the situation was, and finally, how you would handle it now. Most importantly, tell the interviewer why you would handle it differently now – did your previous solution create stress on the relationship with the other person, or do you wish that you had stood up more for what you wanted? While you shouldn't elaborate on how poorly you handled the situation before, the most important thing is to show that you've grown and reached a deeper level of understanding as a result of the conflict.

59: Tell me about a time when you negotiated a conflict between other employees.

Answer:

An especially important question for those interviewing for a supervisory role – begin with a specific situation, and explain how you communicated effectively to each individual. For example, did you introduce a compromise? Did you make an executive decision? Or, did you perform as a mediator and encourage the employees to reach a conclusion on their own?

60: What are the three most important things you're looking for in a position?

Answer:

The top three things you want in a position should be similar to the top three things the employer wants from an employee, so that it is clear that you are well-matched to the job. For example, the employer wants a candidate who is well-qualified for and has practical experience – and you want a position that allows you to use your education and skills to their best applications. The employer wants a candidate who is willing to take on new challenges and develop new systems to increase sales or productivity – and you want a position that pushes you and offers opportunities to develop, create, and lead new initiatives. The employer wants a candidate who will grow into and stay with the company for a long time – and you want a position that offers stability and believes in building a strong team. Research what the employer is looking for beforehand, and match your objectives to theirs.

61: How are you evaluating the companies you're looking to work with?

Answer:

While you may feel uncomfortable exerting your own requirements during the interview, the employer wants to see that you are thinking critically about the companies you're applying with, just as they are critically looking at you. Don't be afraid to specify what your needs from a company are (but do try to make sure they match up well with the company – preferably before you apply there), and show confidence and decisiveness in your answer. The interviewer wants to know that you're the kind of person who knows what they want, and how to get it.

62: Are you comfortable working for _____ salary?

Answer:

If the answer to this question is no, it may be a bit of a deal-breaker in a first interview, as you are unlikely to have much room to negotiate. You can try to leverage a bit by highlighting specific experience you have, and how that makes you qualified for more, but be aware that this is very difficult to navigate at this step of the process. To avoid this situation, be aware of industry standards and, if possible, company standards, prior to your application.

63: Why did you choose your last job?

Answer:

In learning what led you to your last job, the interviewer is able to get a feel for the types of things that motivate you. Keep these professionally-focused, and remain passionate about the early points of your career, and how excited you were to get started in the field.

64: How long has it been since your last job and why?

Answer:

Be sure to have an explanation prepared for all gaps in employment, and make sure it's a professional reason. Don't mention difficulties you may have had in finding a job, and instead focus on positive things such as pursuing outside interests or perhaps returning to school for additional education.

65: What other types of jobs have you been looking for?

Answer:

The answer to this question can show the interviewer that you're both on the market and in demand. Mention jobs you've applied for or looked at that are closely related to your field, or similar to the position you're interviewing for. Don't bring up last-ditch efforts that found you applying for a part-time job completely unrelated to your field.

66: Have you ever been disciplined at work?

Answer:

Hopefully the answer here is no – but if you have been disciplined for something at work though, be absolutely sure that you can explain it thoroughly. Detail what you learned from the situation, and reflect on how you grew after the process.

67: What is your availability like?

Answer:

Your availability should obviously be as open as possible, and any gaps in availability should be explained and accounted for. Avoid asking about vacation or personal days (as well as other benefits), and convey to the interviewer how serious you are about your work.

68: May I contact your current employer?

Answer:

If possible, it is best to allow an interviewer to contact your current employer as a reference. However, if it's important that your employer is not contacted, explain your reason tactfully, such as you just started job searching and you haven't had the opportunity yet to inform them that you are looking for other employment. Be careful of this reasoning though, as employers may wonder if you'll start shopping for something better while employed with them as well.

69: Do you have any valuable contacts you could bring to our business?

Answer:

It's great if you can bring knowledge, references, or other contacts that your new employer may be able to network with. However, be sure that you aren't offering up any of your previous employer's clients, or in any way violating contractual agreements.

70: How soon would you be available to start working?

Answer:

While you want to be sure that you're available to start as soon as possible if the company is interested in hiring you, if you still have another job, be sure to give them at least two weeks' notice. Though your new employer may be anxious for you to start, they will want to hire a worker whom they can respect for giving adequate notice, so that they won't have to worry if you'll eventually leave them in the lurch.

71: Why would your last employer say that you left?

Answer:

The key to this question is that your employer's answer must be the same as your own answer about why you left. For instance, if you've told your employer that you left to find a position with greater opportunities for career advancement, your employer had better not say that you were let go for missing too many days of work. Honesty is key in your job application process.

72: How long have you been actively looking for a job?
Answer:

It's best if you haven't been actively looking for a job for very long, as a long period of time may make the interviewer wonder why no one else has hired you. If it has been awhile, make sure to explain why, and keep it positive. Perhaps you haven't come across many opportunities that provide you with enough of a challenge or that are adequately matched to someone of your education and experience.

73: When don't you show up to work?
Answer:

Clearly, the only time acceptable to miss work is for a real emergency or when you're truly sick – so don't start bringing up times now that you plan to miss work due to vacations or family birthdays. Alternatively, you can tell the interviewer how dedicated to your work you are, and how you always strive to be fully present and to put in the same amount of work every time you come in, even when you're feeling slightly under the weather.

74: What is the most common reason you miss work?

Answer:

If there is a reason that you will miss work routinely, this is the time to disclose it – but doing so during an interview will reflect negatively on you. Ideally, you will only miss work during cases of extreme illness or other emergencies.

75: What is your attendance record like?

Answer:

Be sure to answer this question honestly, but ideally you will have already put in the work to back up the fact that you rarely miss days or arrive late. However, if there are gaps in your attendance, explain them briefly with appropriate reasons, and make sure to emphasize your dedication to your work, and reliability.

76: Where did you hear about this position?

Answer:

This may seem like a simple question, but the answer can actually speak volumes about you. If you were referred by a friend or another employee who works for the company, this is a great chance to mention your connection (if the person is in good standing!). However, if you heard about it from somewhere like a career fair or a work placement agency, you may want to focus on how pleased you were to come across such a wonderful opportunity.

77: Tell me anything else you'd like me to know when making a hiring decision.

Answer:

This is a great opportunity for you to give a final sell of yourself to the interviewer – use this time to remind the interviewer of why you are qualified for the position, and what you can bring to the company that no one else can. Express your excitement for the opportunity to work with a company pursuing X mission.

And Finally Good Luck!

INDEX

CORE JAVA Interview Questions

19: When will you use assertions?

20: How will you use assertion?

21: Which of the following codes are legal?

22: Which of the Java versions support assertion?

23: How will you compile your Java code for assertions?

24: How will you enable and disable assertion for your class during runtime?

25: How will you enable and disable assertion for a package during runtime?

26: What does the below line of code represent?

27: What does the below line of code represent?

28: When to use assertions in public method and when to not? In general, what is the best practice?

Wrapper Classes, Garbage Collection, and Exception Handling

29: What is a Wrapper class in Java? What are the special properties of Wrapper class objects?

30: What will be the output?

31: What is Garbage Collection in Java?

32: Which part of the memory is used in Garbage Collection? Which algorithm does the JVM use for Garbage collection?

33: Can you guarantee or force Garbage Collection? If so explain how?

34: What is the difference between an error and an exception in Java?

35: Explain 'throw', 'throws' and 'Throwable' in Java.

36: Explain the try-catch-finally statement in Java.

37: What is the output?

38: What is the purpose of wrapper classes?

39: What are the wrapper classes available in Java?

40: How will you define Autoboxing with an example?

41: What will be the output when you execute the below code:

60: What will be the output on executing the below mentioned code?

61: What are the exception types that can be thrown using the "throw" keyword?

62: How will you write a compilable code block using "throw" keyword?

Threads

63: Differentiate between a Thread and a Process in Java

64: What are the different types of Thread? Explain

65: What is a deadlock in Java and how do you avoid it?

66: What is the difference between wait() and sleep()?

67: The start() method is usually called in the thread which in turn calls the run() method. Why is usually the run() method called directly?

68: How will you define a Thread?

69: What happens behind the scenes when you execute the below program?

70: How will you create Threads in Java?

71: What are the methods of Thread class that are mainly used to manage threads?

72: How does a thread get executed in Java?

73: What are the thread states?

74: Write a compilable Java code that creates a child thread using "Thread" class.

75: What are the methods of Objects that are used while managing threads?

76: Write a compilable Java code that creates a child thread using "Runnable".

77: Is it possible to create more than one thread in a Java application? If so, how will the threads communicate with each other?

78: How will you define Synchronization?

79: What will happen when you execute the code below?

80: Look at the code below. What will happen when you execute the below code? If it compiles fine, what will be the output?

81: Look at the code below. What will happen when you execute the below code? If it compiles fine, what will be the output?

82: What will be the output for the following code?

83: Look at the code below.

84: How will you make a thread to pause for ten minutes?

85: How will you use the "synchronized" keyword? Give code examples.

86: What happens when a synchronized method is invoked?

87: How will you make the thread to wait and start its execution again so that certain process gets executed?

88: Write a Java code and implement "wait" and "notify" methods.

89: What is a Deadlock?

90: When will Deadlock happen?

91: What are the methods that belong to "Runnable" interface?

92: What is the use of join() and yield() methods?

Object Oriented Programming Concepts

93: What is an Object in software and what are the benefits of Objects?

94: Explain method overloading and method overriding.

95: Explain interface and inheritance.

96: What is a singleton class?

97: State the benefits of Object Orientation.

98: What do you have to do to implement "flexible", "extensible", and "maintainable" code? Give examples.

99: Write a code snippet that uses encapsulation concept.

100: What are the benefits of inheritance?

101: Write a code that uses inheritance concept.

102: What are the types of inheritance relationships?

103: Write a piece of code that implements inheritance relationship.

104: Which is non-polymorphic in Java? State the reasons.

105: What is the benefit of reference variable? Give an example.

106: When we cannot reassign the reference variable to other objects?

107: Is it possible to extend more than one class? State the reasons.

108: How will you assign a reference variable to more than one object?

109: How will you differentiate "overloading" and "overriding"?

110: Write a Java code that does method overriding.

111: Write a Java code that does method overloading?

112: Find the below code.

113: Give examples for illegal method overrides.

114: How will you define a constructor? Give an example.

115: What is the use of constructors?

116: What will be the output when we compile and execute the above code?

117: What is the use of super() and where to use this?

118: What happens when you compile the above code? What is the return type called?

119: What are the possible access modifiers for a constructor?

120: What happens behind the scenes if you do not include a constructor in the class?

121: What happens when you compile the above code?

Declarations and Access Controls

122: You are given an assignment to create a game of Tic Tac Toe using a multi dimensional array. How do you initialize the array?

123: Examine the code given below and explain the result when you compile it.

124: What is the benefit of declaring a class as final?

125: How will you define an Identifier?

126: What are access and non-access modifiers? Give examples.

127: How will you declare a compilable abstract class?

128: How will you declare a method name that follows JavaBean standard?

Java Assignments

152: Which of the following are valid statements?

153: What gets printed on the standard output when the class below is compiled and executed?

154: What is Heap and Stack?

155: Look at the below code:

156: What is a string literal? Give an example.

157: How will you cast an "int" literal to "byte" explicitly? Is it really necessary to cast "int" literal to "byte"?

158: Give an example for implicit cast.

159: Write two lines of code using casting and explain how will you assign a "float" to a "short"?

160: What are the possible ways to assign a "float" literal to a "float" variable?

161: Look at the below code:

162: Look at the below code:

163: How will you define scope and what are the different types of scope in variables?

164: How will you define an Octal and Hexadecimal literal in an "int" variable?

165: What are the possible ways of declaring a "double" literal in a "double" variable?

166: Look at the below code:

167: What is the default value for "Boolean" and "char" type instance variable?

168: What will be the default value of a reference variable when it is not explicitly initialized? How will you handle this in code?

169: Look at the below code:

170: What is the default value for "float", "double", "byte", "short", "int", and "long" type instance varibles?

171: Have a look at the below code:

172: How will you declare a "primitive array" and "reference array"?

194: What will be the output when you compile and execute the code mentioned below?

195: What is a ternary operator? Give an example.

196: What will be the value of "a" and "b" when the below code is executed?

197: State the use of instanceof operator. Give an example.

198: Will the code mentioned below compile? If so, what will be the output?

199: Will the below line of code compile? If so, what will be the value?

200: What happens when you execute the below code?

201: How will you define "^" operator? What is its use?

202: What will be the output on executing the code below?

203: What will be the output of the below line of code? Give explanation.

204: Explain about postfix and prefix operators. Give example.

205: What will be output of the below lines of code? Give explanation.

Inner Classes and String Handling

206: What is the output? Explain

207: What is an inner class? What are the different ways an inner class can be defined?

208: What is the difference between == and equals() in string comparison?

209: What is an Inner class?

210: What are the types of classes available in Java?

211: Write a compilable code that creates an instance of inner class from the outer class.

212: Write two lines of code which will instantiate the inner class from the outer class.

213: Explain about "method-local" inner class.

214: What happens when you compile and execute the following line of code?

215: Explain about anonymous inner class.

216: Write two lines of code and explain how will you implement an anonymous inner class.

217: Explain about Static Nested classes.

218: Write a line of code and explain how will you instantiate the static nested class.

219: Write a program and explain how will you declare method-local inner class.

220: What are the valid modifiers of an inner class?

221: What are the various ways of assigning a string literal to a String variable?

222: Which method is used to append a string literal to a String variable?

223: What will be the output when you compile and execute the following code?

224: What are the most widely used methods of String class?

225: When will you use String class and when will you use StringBuffer?

226: How will you add string to a StringBuffer? Give an example.

227: What will be the output when you compile and execute the following code?

228: What is the difference between StringBuffer and StringBuilder?

229: Which class is preferred : StringBuffer or StringBuilder? Why?

230: How will you assign a string literal in a StringBuilder and print its value from right to left?

231: Is it possible to invoke chained methods in Java? If so, how will you invoke?

232: What will be the value of the string object "yValue" from the below code?

233: Have a look at the below code and explain how many reference variables and how many string objects will be available in the memory?

Streams

234: What are the different methods to create a java stream?

235: What is the difference between streams and collections?

236: What is ParallelStream ?

237: What is a forEach() method used for?

238: What is the use of I/O streams?

239: What happens when you execute the below line of code?

240: Write a code that will create a file in the path /usr/CoreJava.txt.

241: What is the use of File class?

242: What are the important methods of File class that are often used?

243: What is the use of FileReader class?

244: What is the use of FileWriter class?

245: Write a code snippet that writes content in the file /usr/CoreJava.txt, reads the content from that file and displays the output in the console using FileWriter and FileReader.

246: Write two lines of code that create a directory in the local file system.

247: What happens when you compile and execute the code below? What will be the output?

248: What is the use of BufferedReader class?

249: What is the use of BufferedWriter class?

250: Write four lines of code that will write contents in a file using PrintWriter class.

251: Write three lines of code to create and delete a file.

252: Which method is used to change the file name and directory? Give an example.

253: How will you define Serialization?

254: Which methods are used to serialize and de-serialize objects?

255: What is the use of transient keyword?

256: How will you use serialization in your code?

257: What are the methods of Serializable interface?

258: What is the use of ObjectOutputStream?

259: What is the use of ObjectInputStream?

260: What will be the output when you compile the code below?

261: Which of the following lines will compile and which will not?

262: What will be the output of the following code?

Collections

263: What are the four interfaces of Java collections?

264: List the differences between the Iterator and Enumeration interfaces?

265: What are the common algorithms implemented in Collections Framework?

266: Assume that you have added all the employee names that are available in Database to a list. How will you display the employee names in natural order?

267: Explain about Queue interface.

268: Which collection would you choose, if you need to keep track of which employee was last accessed from the collection? Explain about its iteration speed.

269: Which feature of Java is used to convert primitive type to reference type?

270: What are the points you need to remember when you override equals() and compareTo() method?

271: How will you search for a specific element in collection?

272: How will you define a reflexive equals() contract?

273: Which collection would you choose if you want no duplicates and if objects are not stored in an order?

274: How will you use the Comparator interface in your class file?

275: Explain symmetric equals() contract.

276: How will you review the queue of a collection object?

277: Is it possible to mix generic and non-generic collections? If so, give example.

278: Explain transitive equals() contract.

279: What happens when you compile and run the following code?

280: Will the following line of code compile without error? If not, state the reasons.

281: Assume that we have a String array containing five elements. What will be the range of results if we make a search on the string array? State the reasons for the same.

282: Will the following line of code compile without error? If not, state the reasons.

283: Assume that we have a below method

284: What are the activities that can be performed in collection API?

285: In collection, which method is used to remove the head of the queue?

286: Which collection class method is not synchronized but allows growing or shrinking its size and provides indexed access to its elements?

287: How will you define a consistent equals() contract?

288: How will you extract elements from a collection without knowing how the collection is implemented?

289: In collection, which classes and interfaces support event handling?

290: How will you access locale specific resources in Java?

HR Questions

1: Where do you find ideas?

2: How do you achieve creativity in the workplace?

3: How do you push others to create ideas?

4: Describe your creativity.

5: Would you rather receive more authority or more responsibility at work?

6: What do you do when someone in a group isn't contributing their fair share?

7: Tell me about a time when you made a decision that was outside of your authority.

8: Are you comfortable going to supervisors with disputes?

9: If you had been in charge at your last job, what would you have done differently?

10: Do you believe employers should praise or reward employees for a job well done?

11: What do you believe is the most important quality a leader can have?

12: Tell me about a time when an unforeseen problem arose. How did you handle it?

13: Can you give me an example of a time when you were able to improve X objective at your previous job?

14: Tell me about a time when a supervisor did not provide specific enough direction on a project.

15: Tell me about a time when you were in charge of leading a project.

16: Tell me about a suggestion you made to a former employer that was later implemented.

17: Tell me about a time when you thought of a way something in the workplace could be done more efficiently.

18: Is there a difference between leading and managing people – which is your greater strength?

19: Do you function better in a leadership role, or as a worker on a team?

20: Tell me about a time when you discovered something in the workplace that was disrupting your (or others) productivity – what did you do about it?

21: How do you perform in a job with clearly-defined objectives and goals?

22: How do you perform in a job where you have great decision-making power?

23: If you saw another employee doing something dishonest or unethical, what would you do?

24: Tell me about a time when you learned something on your own that later helped in your professional life.

25: Tell me about a time when you developed a project idea at work.

26: Tell me about a time when you took a risk on a project.

27: What would you tell someone who was looking to get into this field?

28: Tell me about a time when you didn't meet a deadline.

29: How do you eliminate distractions while working?

30: Tell me about a time when you worked in a position with a weekly or monthly quota to meet. How often were you successful?

31: Tell me about a time when you met a tough deadline, and how you were able to complete it.

32: How do you stay organized when you have multiple projects on your plate?

33: How much time during your work day do you spend on "auto-pilot?"

34: How do you handle deadlines?

35: Tell me about your personal problem-solving process.

36: What sort of things at work can make you stressed?

37: What do you look like when you are stressed about something? How do you solve it?

38: Can you multi-task?

39: How many hours per week do you work?

40 How many times per day do you check your email?

position?

61: How are you evaluating the companies you're looking to work with?

62: Are you comfortable working for _____ salary?

63: Why did you choose your last job?

64: How long has it been since your last job and why?

65: What other types of jobs have you been looking for?

66: Have you ever been disciplined at work?

67: What is your availability like?

68: May I contact your current employer?

69: Do you have any valuable contacts you could bring to our business?

70: How soon would you be available to start working?

71: Why would your last employer say that you left?

72: How long have you been actively looking for a job?

73: When don't you show up to work?

74: What is the most common reason you miss work?

75: What is your attendance record like?

76: Where did you hear about this position?

77: Tell me anything else you'd like me to know when making a hiring decision

Some of the following titles might also be handy:

1. .NET Interview Questions You'll Most Likely Be Asked
2. 200 Interview Questions You'll Most Likely Be Asked
3. Access VBA Programming Interview Questions You'll Most Likely Be Asked
4. Adobe ColdFusion Interview Questions You'll Most Likely Be Asked
5. Advanced Excel Interview Questions You'll Most Likely Be Asked
6. Advanced JAVA Interview Questions You'll Most Likely Be Asked
7. Advanced SAS Interview Questions You'll Most Likely Be Asked
8. AJAX Interview Questions You'll Most Likely Be Asked
9. Algorithms Interview Questions You'll Most Likely Be Asked
10. Android Development Interview Questions You'll Most Likely Be Asked
11. Ant & Maven Interview Questions You'll Most Likely Be Asked
12. Apache Web Server Interview Questions You'll Most Likely Be Asked
13. Artificial Intelligence Interview Questions You'll Most Likely Be Asked
14. ASP.NET Interview Questions You'll Most Likely Be Asked
15. Automated Software Testing Interview Questions You'll Most Likely Be Asked
16. Base SAS Interview Questions You'll Most Likely Be Asked
17. BEA WebLogic Server Interview Questions You'll Most Likely Be Asked
18. C & C++ Interview Questions You'll Most Likely Be Asked
19. C# Interview Questions You'll Most Likely Be Asked
20. C++ Internals Interview Questions You'll Most Likely Be Asked
21. CCNA Interview Questions You'll Most Likely Be Asked
22. Cloud Computing Interview Questions You'll Most Likely Be Asked
23. Computer Architecture Interview Questions You'll Most Likely Be Asked
24. Computer Networks Interview Questions You'll Most Likely Be Asked
25. CORE JAVA Interview Questions You'll Most Likely Be Asked
26. Data Structures & Algorithms Interview Questions You'll Most Likely Be Asked
27. Data WareHousing Interview Questions You'll Most Likely Be Asked
28. EJB 3.0 Interview Questions You'll Most Likely Be Asked
29. Entity Framework Interview Questions You'll Most Likely Be Asked
30. Fedora & RHEL Interview Questions You'll Most Likely Be Asked
31. GNU Development Interview Questions You'll Most Likely Be Asked
32. Hibernate, Spring & Struts Interview Questions You'll Most Likely Be Asked
33. HTML, XHTML and CSS Interview Questions You'll Most Likely Be Asked
34. HTML5 Interview Questions You'll Most Likely Be Asked
35. IBM WebSphere Application Server Interview Questions You'll Most Likely Be Asked
36. iOS SDK Interview Questions You'll Most Likely Be Asked
37. Java / J2EE Design Patterns Interview Questions You'll Most Likely Be Asked
38. Java / J2EE Interview Questions You'll Most Likely Be Asked
39. Java Messaging Service Interview Questions You'll Most Likely Be Asked
40. JavaScript Interview Questions You'll Most Likely Be Asked
41. JavaServer Faces Interview Questions You'll Most Likely Be Asked
42. JDBC Interview Questions You'll Most Likely Be Asked
43. jQuery Interview Questions You'll Most Likely Be Asked
44. JSP-Servlet Interview Questions You'll Most Likely Be Asked
45. JUnit Interview Questions You'll Most Likely Be Asked
46. Linux Commands Interview Questions You'll Most Likely Be Asked
47. Linux Interview Questions You'll Most Likely Be Asked
48. Linux System Administrator Interview Questions You'll Most Likely Be Asked
49. Mac OS X Lion Interview Questions You'll Most Likely Be Asked
50. Mac OS X Snow Leopard Interview Questions You'll Most Likely Be Asked

51. Microsoft Access Interview Questions You'll Most Likely Be Asked
52. Microsoft Excel Interview Questions You'll Most Likely Be Asked
53. Microsoft Powerpoint Interview Questions You'll Most Likely Be Asked
54. Microsoft Word Interview Questions You'll Most Likely Be Asked
55. MySQL Interview Questions You'll Most Likely Be Asked
56. NetSuite Interview Questions You'll Most Likely Be Asked
57. Networking Interview Questions You'll Most Likely Be Asked
58. OOPS Interview Questions You'll Most Likely Be Asked
59. Operating Systems Interview Questions You'll Most Likely Be Asked
60. Oracle DBA Interview Questions You'll Most Likely Be Asked
61. Oracle E-Business Suite Interview Questions You'll Most Likely Be Asked
62. ORACLE PL/SQL Interview Questions You'll Most Likely Be Asked
63. Perl Programming Interview Questions You'll Most Likely Be Asked
64. PHP Interview Questions You'll Most Likely Be Asked
65. PMP Interview Questions You'll Most Likely Be Asked
66. Python Interview Questions You'll Most Likely Be Asked
67. RESTful JAVA Web Services Interview Questions You'll Most Likely Be Asked
68. Ruby Interview Questions You'll Most Likely Be Asked
69. Ruby on Rails Interview Questions You'll Most Likely Be Asked
70. SAP ABAP Interview Questions You'll Most Likely Be Asked
71. SAP HANA Interview Questions You'll Most Likely Be Asked
72. SAS Programming Guidelines Interview Questions You'll Most Likely Be Asked
73. Selenium Testing Tools Interview Questions You'll Most Likely Be Asked
74. Silverlight Interview Questions You'll Most Likely Be Asked
75. Software Repositories Interview Questions You'll Most Likely Be Asked
76. Software Testing Interview Questions You'll Most Likely Be Asked
77. SQL Server Interview Questions You'll Most Likely Be Asked
78. Tomcat Interview Questions You'll Most Likely Be Asked
79. UML Interview Questions You'll Most Likely Be Asked
80. Unix Interview Questions You'll Most Likely Be Asked
81. UNIX Shell Programming Interview Questions You'll Most Likely Be Asked
82. VB.NET Interview Questions You'll Most Likely Be Asked
83. Windows Server 2008 R2 Interview Questions You'll Most Likely Be Asked
84. XLXP, XSLT, XPATH, XFORMS & XQuery Interview Questions You'll Most Likely Be Asked
85. XML Interview Questions You'll Most Likely Be Asked

For complete list visit

www.vibrantpublishers.com

NOTES

Made in the USA
San Bernardino, CA
01 May 2018